Visibility

for Maggie

Visibility

New and Selected Poems

Graham Mort

seren

seren
is the book imprint of
Poetry Wales Press Ltd
57 Nolton Street, Bridgend, Wales, CF31 3AE
www.seren-books.com

The right of Graham Mort to be identified as
the Author of this Work has been asserted in accordance
with the Copyright, Designs and Patents Act, 1988.

ISBN 1-85411-439-6

A CIP record for this title is available from the British Library.

The publisher acknowledges the financial assistance
of the Welsh Books Council.

Printed by Bell & Bain, Glasgow

CONTENTS

Visibility

A Country on Fire/Sky Burial

Snow from the North

Circular Breathing

A Night on the Lash

VISIBILITY

THE FETCHING

I was at the fetching of the sea:
it brought white waves to harry me.

Then the fetching of the wind that
brought the sea to lick earth's rind.

I was at the fetching of the stars that
brought the years to salt our tears.

Then the fetching of the souls the sea
had beached in bitter pools.

I was at the fetching of the Gulf that
brought the oil that loosed the wolf.

Then the fetching of the war that
lost those souls for evermore.

I was at the fetching of the times
when trust decayed as flesh in lime.

And so the fetching of the fears that
brought the dark that still is here.

The fetching of words is worse: since
killing tainted them the poem is cursed.

A SWALLOW MAYBE

It falls into the orchard's
    expectancy
from Africa's parted
    veil of heat
a blue knot of lightning
    splintered from icy
stratospheres
    surprising the
suddenly crackling grass

then slants between
    trunks of pear trees
mossy and ingrown
    sparking between
pylons and power lines
    their toxic chitter
their stanzas of unformed
    consonants

it turns our heads'
    heliotrope bloom
of astonishment
    unpinning its brooch
of lapis from
    the afternoon
a foil for certainties
    that steer into dusk –
those oyster catchers
    pronouncing
the salt-dazed mirage
    of the estuary

now it is flown into
    the copse like war
its red throat silently
    booming and aflame
scattering wood sorrel

into the gloom
shy and self-amazed

its cry is high-wired
    drawn beyond anvils
to the thinnest
    highest
most inhuman note
    on which it vibrates
ululates
    vanishes
between the synapses
    of our eyes:

a thought split
    between us
unfinished
    lost maybe
or never
    happening.

DITHYRAMB

We lie on our backs in the bright field
of the poem, listening to the hum of
the earth, the indecipherable language
of magnetism; it spins us like needles
as as we watch the burst blue sofa
of the sky. Everything is rich and dizzy
in the poem: syllables fizz and wasps
fly to the petals of our faces to drink
sweet spit. The sun goes down behind
torched cities and we look beyond the sky
to where the Universe must be: a wheel
of whitest incandescent gas that whirls
us into everlastingness. We sleep and
wake up, still inside our lost selves, still
in the poem, still in the night. Blackthorn
blossom covers us, falling from branches
where sloes will ripen a purple bloom of
bitterness. There is a grove of yew trees
dark with Druid's breath, a tomb with
faded writing, an owl coughing, drifts
of pink cherry flowers – the usual corny
stuff of verse. Something quite ordinary
has gone missing in this poem – like rain,
an old brown coin, a day of the week or
punctuation or life – we'll never guess.
Wind is pressing us into wet grass, still
on our backs, still with berry-stained
fingers, so that our hands almost touch:
now a syllable
        now a dactyl
            now a dithyramb
                apart.

GRACIAS

Wind in the lime trees rousing
    a sappy green,
the mountain's dazzling
    scree of white.
Fishermen hoisting a shroud
    the shoal's dulled
phosphorescence
    spilling onto ice.
Flies at the donkey's ancient
    eyes; ardent girls on
mopeds; old men blackened
    by tides of sun blowing
smoke from French cigarettes
    into a Spanish sky.
The road leading us onwards
    or astray; clouds simmering,
the sea's siesta ruffled; a
    mewling squall of cats
that fucked or fought
    all night; an Alsatian
bitch dragging at her mooring
    chain. Those fishing boats
rocking at the quay,
    the church whitewashed in
agonies of light; Christ
    martyred in leaded glass,
all stains washed away
    by one night's simple rain.
Thin birds scream over
    masts, old men, a donkey's
blindness, a restless dog,
    the salt-encrusting sea;
our sins redeemed by swifts'
    near-colliding specks of light.
Your hand on mine, smaller
    than I remember, this *vino tinto*
dusty at our lips, this grace
    of living here and now, this
gratitude: *gracias*.

INDIGO

Today we woke in the ether of indigo: the
    scent of my first jeans near black and
stiff as sails and cool for once in '68 – this
    cotton throw bought late one day in Kano
where slaves were sold a lifetime ago. Trade
    winds and cowries and the sword unfurled its
quintessence of oldest-glowing darkest blue.

Nigerian sun liquefies that memory to a
    blinding yard where children gathered
barefoot and curious to see the white man
    watch their fathers work the dye pits
sucking their teeth to draw each steeping
    piece from sunken lungs for air to stain
its elemental earth-breath blue.

The men watched for what I might do
    or buy or say; a woman laughed in Hausa
covered her face from this rich stranger
    so quiet inside his pale of Englishness;
the Emir's cavalry rode past on Arab mares
    their sinew knotted taut as heat where
benzene vendors haggled in the road.

How could I say I wanted only to watch
    them lift each dusky sky-patch purpling
their red gloves to the wrist? Not to buy or
    be troubled by wealth – except the riches of
light sinking on the city's ochre walls – but to sit
    in shadow as cloth rose and fell in their fists;
all held in the scorched palm of the sun.

What was I thinking? I should have remembered
    the chill here, how the stove is raked and lit
how we're undone each day by seeping cold
    waking to north country rain rinsing green hills
beyond this attic room where breath casts mist

into early day the way I've seen the
sun burn fogs of equatorial night.

Now I'm drowsing in this old scent of Africa,
    new Levis, unexpected youth, vestigial
warmth, those memories soaked in past days.
    Or maybe I'm still asleep, not yet changed by
Africa or chemistry of indigo, the cloth I brought
    thrown back from body-heat where you were
sleeping a second or a century ago.

JACKDAWS

They flock above the stone spike of the church, hunch
at the emerald tips of pines in monkish caps;
their feathers clog the air like silt.

Through weeks of sleet days scattered them to here;
they'll build in our chimney next. Their dry coughs drop
to kitchens, sicken us with hurt or guilt.

Some raise a brood and leave, some fall to hearths – a
blaze of soot. Balaclava'd lags, stoical through smoke,
odds-on scavengers, they stick it out.

All through the night you'll hear them roost, each family
squabbling, unhappily unique, shifting their
heavy theorems from throat to throat.

All winter we forgot how they survived when thinnest on the
land; now they exact reckoning. The kind let slip,
that dereliction breeds the more.

We never thought they'd wait, squat the republic of our
roof, biding there like facts, their kind of
patience stark as poverty or war.

It teaches an attenuated hope, the way they future
on the darkest days, the earth's rotation sussed
through long-additions of the light.

Now we'll face what's left undone or sent the way of hell:
these grumbling sweats are juries of an ancient state
cut from the fabric of the night.

LEARNING TO LIE

In our house by the railway track I learned
to lie – that huge-toothed Blüthner cost
me all my innocence.

Five-finger exercises in the afternoons; white
on black, rote-memoried prayer, my hands'
chance placing on the keys.

Sneers at the window from so-called friends:
the Cotton Belt's brute instinct shamed us
framed in miseries.

Botched chords, that walnut reliquary
resonating, my fingers fluttering the way
wild birds are limed and snared.

We children played from duty's fear and
now don't play. Not one of us could
face that rotten jaw of ivory,

most afternoons dared skip the deadly
hour; the discord and deceit of Easy
Pieces fattened there.

To fox you, we'd angle the piano stool, leave
music thumbed in disarray to figure staves
pored over in harmonic toil.

I learned to lie and how lies serve us in the end –
spoil, necrotise and kill the taste for
things we might have loved.

In music shops I've found the tunes you played
on Sunday nights and sometimes wept
for all that waste.

No guilt: not that. I never wanted your Germanic
airs, chose Sonny Boy over Chopin,
Leadbelly over Liszt.

I knew by heart what stymied yours: missed
education; put to work then war; the Blitz,
the years of blancoed bullshit

fighting for an England that was never ours.
You played for officers, amazing them
with flattened vowels and fluencies

of touch before they went to die, oiled-up on France's
sand; choked hopes left music raging at
the bars of everything beyond.

Late teens, I found an old Braille radio, its
dial ironic when Alabama boys were blind,
its stations stuttering out of true to

fish a Mississippi flood's benighted shoal:
gospel songs and delta blues – those
struck-steel choruses spurring

me to make my first half-playable guitar, break
bottle necks, find open chords, Spanish
tuning sweet as sherry dregs.

I let that glass throat on my aching finger sing:
not much like Elmore James, but close
to the sob and whine, the static hum

and heat of Louisiana nights I'd heard when
valves glowed through the throb of
haunted sleep or sleeplessness.

Locos shunted sparks to the hobo dark they
towed between decaying towns, making
the roof slates shake, the piano

downstairs thrum its walking bass – a freight
train's woman-hungry, lonesome
north-of-England blues.

That memory takes me closest to a kind of truth
I've been. Not right or wrong – the way, as
Armstrong said, you've got to love

to play. And sometimes how love's wasted
when it should find reciprocity or
temperament in song.

Illusions? Slick tuning tricks to cram in memory's
scale? Maybe. The space between us
now's all clashing undertones.

Perhaps we'll voice it once before you die:
how chords put intervals in harmony and
sequences resolve like darkness

closing day. Maybe we'll share one glorious
dawn of dissonance where lies
find truth another way.

JUNIPER

Serra de Tramuntana

Hike over scree, through holm oak and
Aleppo pines above the almond grove
at the valley head to reach this cave.

Its goat-scented shadow is bitten
from an orange rind of stone to face
the purple plains, a drowsing sea.

A line of karabiners gropes across the
roof, a low wall shelters kids in spring
and now fends out the sun.

Bird cries, snagged wings, the crack of
pine cones in resin-ethered air: one
spark would vent *siroccos* of flame.

Stand where the curious dead have
always stood, drawn from the valley to
understand this entry to the dark,

gazing through sweat and missed
heartbeats towards the unsafe sea,
its new tongues sculling in

to name a dry season
or sudden autumn rain
or juniper.

AIRPLANE

Doing microsurgery on an airline meal,
a stranger's elbow in your face, nothing
seems real, or what it seems appears
sparse as leg room, personal space.

You gaze, pressurised and calm. The
Alps go by in snow; a chain of lakes;
sea, salt flats, dunes, a river threading
fabricated nation states below.

The plane tracks an electronic map – its
guess at where we are unscaled – a steward
brings hot towels, chilled water in a tub.
Water, you think, could save the world.

Then dusky minarets of cloud above
wind-stirred sheaves of desert thorn; the
muezzin's zones of light are left behind
for night under a horn of moon.

You cinch your belt through turbulence
drench thirst in sips, then sleep sus-
pended in false atmosphere, tracked
by your own heart's radar beep.

A good way to die, nocturnal flight that
leaves the sun lagging in its arc; embalmed
by altitude you wake to runway lights,
touch down like thunder from the dark.

DRINKING THE MOTORCYCLE

Tonight we're drinking the motorcycle; last year
the camper van; last week the piano, hammer
by hammer, string by string.

Today I dealt with a man who stank of grease, his
fingers black with honesty of oil. *A deal*, he
said, thumbing the wadded blur of cash.

Tonight we'll start with carburetors, the butterfly choke,
a glass of long-stemmed inlet valves before we grope
to bed drunk on the flywheel's timing marks.

You lean from a window, tell the street we're drinking the
poet's motorcycle; I sit with a glass of fork-oil, yearn
for its damping effect, for lost pistons in nickel

alloy barrels, con-rods and crankshaft, the helical drive in
its hemisphere of gears. I'll sob for clutch-plate and
pressure plate, for floating bush and sliding dog.

Tonight I'll dream of spark plugs purged of their black
humours: the grief and loss of mistimed strokes.
Recidivist, I'll weep regret and watch

the road recede. Last week you cried for the piano's sonatas
and preludes: every glass of Chopin, every hint of
Bartok rising in the bouquet's notes.

Now we're drinking a motorcycle: its exhaust baffles,
its nocturne of softly throbbing light, its miles
of anywhere, the darklit road ahead.

Grenache chills my hands like headwind near journey's
end where the spokes and sidestand find repose;
now a toast to rocker covers, relays

and well-set points, to the engine's paean of bronze
and heated oil; let's rise to celebrate the hypoid
of the bevel drive, the dark lube of the sump.

Encore to the brakes' hydraulic pads and polished disks!
Nature hates a vacuum: soon we'll be drunk, redlining
its canticle of parts. She'll tell upstarers in the

street we're right to drink, regretting every drop. Today, I
dealt with a man who thumbed a hurtling emptiness;
the slipstream of all loss is smeared in ink.

BAT VALLEY, KAMPALA

You'll hear grasshoppers kindle their song, scratching
under palms beyond the mosque's gilt minaret where
slippers line up pale as lilies closing at the dusk.

Let's say a storm still billows at the western hills; there'll
be clouds of saffron bile, the sky fused-out, short-
circuiting in flickering blue effulgent sparks.

Roosting fruit bats flit from trees, loot last light, fly
from thunder's heat-charged columns to the sun-
spilled crimson of the lake's sheen.

The sky stammers bats: a host of sable tents,
torrent of invert light; their flux of dark spews
shadow on a dimming township's red dirt roads.

Sky sputters. The market breathes its scent of burnt
earth, plantain rot and diesel smoke, the cheeks of
maize-cob vendors etched by candles where you walk.

You watch those boys fade from the tennis court, returning
their lost ball when only bats should sense it scuffing
home from scooped half-volleys in the dusk.

They shake hands, slam their iron cage: *Go well*. The sky's
still flocculent with wings, the night a broth of dog howls,
storm-heat, sweat and insect-crackling grass.

Mosquitos blacken window mesh; moths' giant shadows
beat the lawn. Another drink: the glass cold, beer sharp
as constellations drawing current from the dark.

BIRTHDAYS IN SPAIN

A sea-breeze sets itself between
your teeth, lifts a strand of thinning
hair, freckles your arms where fair
skin shines with easy health.

The bay a dab of paint, spray falling,
rocks scabbed with shit and feathers,
swifts cursive, transcribing the air's
faint whisper and hum.

Anointed with factor 40, sea-water's
gush of clarity, she slips on shingle
and you catch her. A wave chases
her scream to the shore. Life is full:

ensemadas and coffee, apricots in
a wooden bowl, the card she tucked
into a novel as a gift; her lips, the pull
of August days strutting in leonine heat.

Days hotter than you remember, seas
higher; things shrinking, deepening,
an absence of ice. A gull's scream
drowns that inner howl.

Her father's last trip. Shirtsleeved, he
scans *The Times*. His eyes are stones
fading from sea's wash of sky – its
lack of haste almost surprising,

its lick of salt already dry.

QUIETUDE

1. Conjugation

Gazing at Scots cattle in a
 Welsh valley those coy red-
heads shunting steam
 towards an orange-tinctured
dawn where squirrels ghost
 the treeline – twin
tongues of smoke
 snagged scarves – flickering
from twigs that tremble to
 conduct their hardly-pausing
weightlessness touching
 and balancing a nanosecond
quicker than I can register it
 or know that when they broke
cover to climb the sky the
 thought I had of them was
next to something else – its
 shadow swimming under iced
grey water then rising through
 spurned crystal to image her –
my mother
hunched white-haired
 and hemmed in deafened
puzzlement of place and why
 she's there or which hapless
son I am come to visit her
 from the driveway with its
wax snowdrops ash buds
 and crocus spears
or from the road which
 took me here where I am
still somehow myself
 hacking frost with my heels
a winter morning's hawthorn
 berries she'd have loved
ripening from the passing
 tense I'm walking through

2. *Vocation*

It was you taught me the names
  for things: the difference between
a couple or a few, nettle sting from
  chamomile, sky from earth, all
compass points, rivers, train from
  track, roads from lanes, how hand
in hand could keep us safe. That hoard
  of words seems new still, leads me
back, brightens a dusk of everlasting
  past to memory's lit space. Out
of nothingness its golden flare – late
  autumn gorse where words cross-
pollinate this consciousness that
  cannot last. Pain glows there, too,
its brand of sentience pricing life too
  high. Now you must teach me how
to die. I'll learn it well I promise. The
  gaze askance, half smiles when
water's raised to moisten speech.
  The way you say *don't look so*
worried! in this place where everyone
  is old. You're showing me a new
vocation: how to ease in quietude,
  how to be bold and reach and take
your hands in mine, thin and blue as
  days recalled. Your deafness makes
the lesson more than half one-way.
  What's left is touch, the merest
pressure of the hand's old brogue. It's
  faint as intercepted Morse the way
you say *let go* – fading inflection of a finger
  on my palm – before you sink towards
all that's unpronounceable and still
  and beyond harm

3. Dyson

I'm Dysoning the old
    house
    hoovering up
    my mother
    with this new verb
Her white hairs in
    the carpet
    her skin scales
    entering the vortex
    with dust mites
    cobwebs
    grit from the street
Now specs of talc
    its mica the glittering
    nebulae
    of the new
    universe she entered.
Even her deafness seems
    gathered here from worn
    carpets and rugs into
    a layered silence
What archaeology
    what a way to
    gather up the dead
    this brown floss spun
    into a Perspex tube!
I don't sing much
    as I work
    the house too quiet
    my father watching me
But think how the world spins
    how it whirls
    abrades
    showers us like sparks
And how we die and how
    the Dyson mingles us
        a family again.

SLOW RIVER TO IRAQ

River is taking it slow
the sun is hardly up
washing a few cars a white
wall water is low a dipper
preens its linen bib Starlings
call taking off their cousins –
comics in the eaves' music
hall A few mayflies circle
where we walk scrawled by
light's gold nib Saucers of
dirty foam go by go with the
flow the river falls over seismic
fractures (though we don't talk)
brown peat-water over broken
stone It's late summer and
we woke numb stunned
apart by the night by thoughts
of England's squalid war
that rise between us sometimes
like a current we're caught in
I'd rather be alone than dumb
That's my face my eyes the river
goes over/through Today even the
kingfisher's subliminal glimpse
of blue can't be agreed on as
real or happening or true
The other face the face that's
drowned in history's grief
the face that's turned away
is you

VISIBILITY

Your boots level with my eyes, slog ahead ankled
in peat, the cold-pressed oils of heather filling
each print with petrol blue.

Later, on the ridge of Ben Dubhcraig, they fill
with nothingness, altitude's aridity, the space
between themselves.

Midges sup at our fraternal blood, clouds
scarf us in chiffon, the gill
chokes underground.

Skylarks will not sing, flitting from rock to
invisibility, unzipping a glimpse of the
lochan flinching below.

A raven near the summit rattles out
the rubric of scree from its
parched throat.

Then the omen of our own caught breath,
your boots chanting their psalm of loss
through rain.

Now voices chink from mist, pass close,
the tongue's stanzas fallen into
stonechat gutturals.

We're lost. Each compass point relative
to where we think we are.
Climb higher, you say.

The needle scrambles sense, spins us
into bluffs that stand from slow
uncertainties of cloud.

Higher towards the gods of mist, towards
bog cotton ghosts luminous as flames;
higher to where this light falls

    almost uselessly
             from heaven.

SUMMER CLOCKS

First blackbirds surround the house, trading
licks, melodic cadences, improvising a febrile
joy over the throbbing scent of lilac, the crack
of heat-warped boards, paint cans popping
in the shed, sun stripping windowsills
and doors to wood's white grain.

She'd been gone a week. A month. Forever.
He couldn't remember. Except that she'd
become provisional – stirring sugar into coffee,
gazing across dumb breakfasts of toast
and heather honey – conditional on other
things, half known or half forgotten.

She thought she'd made herself clear, but
he saw a fine sediment in her eyes when she
tilted her head or swore at the bathroom door
he hid behind, stroking that vein on his arm,
listening to blackbirds, the slow fulfilling sex
of water clucking in a pipe.

Then waking in the empty house: alone in
the kitchen stashing empties, fishing a tea bag
from his cup, sucking at the day's first cigarette,
noticing the clock at ten-to-eight: that sense
of being early, on top, ahead (of things), in
charge of his diurnal destiny.

The clock's been stuck for days, battery
down, hands flicking like something dying
in a web. He's slinging dregs, stubbing smoke,
remembering the rush of dread that says he's
late for work and on a final warning now.
All this is relative, like walking towards

something when walking away, retreating
when actually approaching, time's curve
taking him back or forwards to itself. Today
he's running for a bus. Tomorrow he sets her
place again. She cat-licks in the bathroom;
he smokes; the birds take it away.

WEEKEND COTTAGE

Halt-timbered, remote enough to stall our
car on rutted clay, sunk into a valley's
gorge of streams that dry March hushed
to whispers straying on the land.

We brought the rain. They moaned, as if we'd
hexed them, unlocked the house, stamped
mud, struck a fire, sighed at things we
couldn't guess, and left.

The rooms were stale as still air in a borrowed
house could be. The television new, walls
chrome-yellow in self-conscious gaiety,
the balked oak massive as a ship's.

Look at the butterflies, you said, showing me
admirals waking at the casements, thrashing
flawed glass as if the light and quiet rain
were sugar crystallising there.

Maybe smoke from the ingle-nook bothered
them, brought back from sleep, roused
from the pupae, sloughing off their
first, prefigured death.

Months of frost had tacked their tapestry
against elm doors, behind webbed
panes, until the day we lifted them
by folded wings to set them free.

The light seemed quick to fail, sinking behind
the hill-fort to a dusk of chanting birches,
bleating ewes and buds purpled
at the season's brink.

We let them out to test the cold, winter still
sluggish in their flight. Even skylarks hailing
ramparts snagged in gorse couldn't quite
convince that this was spring.

Maybe we shouldn't have come, you said as
smoke poured blue as sheaves of iris flung
into the room, the air stirring in our throats
to shape whatever might be left to say.

SHAVING SOLILOQUY

Today I'm shaving with a dead man's kit – your
father's razor salvaged from that Catholic council
estate house into rapprochement of a kind.

We bury him today. So now these rites: a clean
shirt, my coat laid out, the day suitably dark, this
6:00 am rising for the long drive south.

A gale barges at the window, wind north-north-west,
scattered rain, the blade taking in my face the way
it quartered every line of his.

All this closeness we never shared: our quarrel
glaciated years of silence until a truce of
Bushmills thawed our tongues.

The basin's scummed with copper, blade rinsed,
brush snug in the chrome tin he used
each morning on the Watford line

shaving in water tapped from the loco, the fire-
man cracking eggs onto a shovel, hurling
optimistic Kildare curses at the dawn.

Which reminds me of the time I shaved a dead
man in asylum sheets; short on mortuary tags, I
did calligraphy on each foot's yellow sole.

Poor lunatic, already long forgotten in that place. Now
there's blood in the foam, someone else's eyes
in the chasm of thought that put them there.

The wafer and the wine of Christ will pass me by,
clenched against the one true faith. Instead,
this ritual: fumbled, uncertain, secular.

MAGDELENE

First light brightens a cockerel's rusted throat;
then Magdelene brushing the terrace, shooing
dust, bougainvillea blossom and leaves fallen
from the lemon tree.

You'd think she'd made the valley like this –
the valley and its scourge of rainlessness –
but she is only brushing away the sins
of the world.

She stops to stare at me. She has a pursed
smile for the priest, a glare for the goat hobbled
in the olive grove, a sigh for bees syringing
nectar from jasmine.

Neither old nor young, she reads the sea
spread between peach-coloured pinnacles
of stone: cool blue, before the sun
turns up its heat.

This is where blossom falls without wind –
and carob leaves and the gnawed rind
of mandarins; this is how the battle-gear
of ants gets swept away

and always how the day begins:
Magdelene, chasing away the night's
shadow, stifling murder in the goat's
chained hooves.

ADVERTISING EXECUTIVE WITH
SPARROWHAWK

This morning the lane was laced with frost,
its glow of leaves curled brandy snaps
falling from the trees.

Clouds, black and gilt-edged. A headful of
Scotch. St. Vitus hands, the thought of
office treachery uppermost.

Dawn's crucible melting the slag of night, the
Saab retching to the road towards another
day of innuendo and damned lies.

Then the sparrowhawk straddling a dove
ambushed from the blackthorn hedge –
one moment coasting the wind

towards all that's ripe and good in life,
the next shafted by some grey-backed
bastard gliding up behind.

The dove lay scuttled, oozing its jewellery
of blood, the hawk glared at me – mere
meat – and only just too big to take.

I thought of how the meek are clutched
by death, the way the hawk felt nothing
good for any living thing, then

how it strutted, stared, flew up quiet as
smoke, chest barred with rage, its eyes
so hard they dented mine.

I changed gear, watched the moon trying
to haunt the day; the engine warm
and purling, needles on the

fascia taut, the car wheels humming
past a badger's mess of spilled-up
guts. Another day. I'll tick it off

tonight, drinking to forget slogans and
video spools and younger, smarter men.
All that seemed so real until then –

that moment of the dove's scattered life,
the hawk staking its claim before crows in
dark suits did their job of aftercare.

But maybe I'll remember how this copse I
drive by every day was melting in the sun;
how I stopped to smoke and sat

here, outside words; watched mist dripping
from the trees, imagined how this hush
must always be here, like the birds.

LABOURER AT KOLOLO

He is cutting stones, the red soil of Kololo;
his blood a heated blade, his palms pale
with sweat in the Kampala sun.

He slices weeds, a crust of earth, the old
hide of empires, the panga's blurred steel
flensing steam-heated air.

He counts hours, then years: rainy seasons
on an iron roof, cassava crops, the sun's
stare through slashed matoke leaves.

Black kites float in the depth of his eye, scavenging
a white-scorched sky; a marabou stork flaps
the drumskin of its hunger.

After noon's vertical sun thunder clouds will plume
those seven knolls, boiling from afternoon heat
into crazed night-time rain.

He stares to the lake's mist, to hills where Kabakas
pitched their courts until death wrapped another
jawbone in barkcloth and silence.

A beetle pincers a grub, its buffed armour scurries
over the man's bare feet, earth's rusted promise,
the broken stones of his labour.

JIHAD

Don't ask me if this is my friend's enemy or my enemy's
friend, this fox with its fanatic eyes slinking at stone walls
where conifers drape the dark and dip in restless breaths
of wind; this fox with nose held high to gauge each nuance
of the gloom, head lasered by its own bright stare.

Drizzle smokes in the headlights, the engine pants. I've
braked the car but the fox won't move. Its coat is brown
in the rain, not red the way a fox is in a storybook or fable.
Its tail is carried low to scuff away tracks through larch
needle humus of the night-time woods.

The radio brings a new kind of war – tells me why the West
is dangered now, though I don't get uniqueness here when
war is death and death is old. Wipers bleat and whirr, smearing
glass, stretching a film of oil to a thinning lie. Then that
tune I can't forget: *I get along without you very well*, its

unsung words keeping time with blades on a windscreen
wet with rain. Insinuations of the night hold me here in the
fox's unironic mullah's glare. He walks away, slips me to
his memory of vixen musk and other kills: a whiff of petrol,
a blurred face, the engine's rasping breath, pale hands at

the wheel which he allows to pass. No more. He'll watch the
pricked blood of my taillights dwindle, the plantation shoulder
its cape of dark, rain needle undergrowth, embroidering its
fatal text. The fox hurdles headlines, finesses frequencies,
rides that song in his own breaking wave of fear.

His gaze returns to spike false sleep where I turn in
half truths, half remembered. Now pausing, now sniffing
the larch-scented night, ears pricked, brush stiffening, all
senses turning in that gimballed head to lock onto the
hare upwind that hasn't yet imagined it must die.

FLASHBACKS

Wild garlic breaking in the wood, its surf
    of musk sweating a damp-scented lust.

A cat's face streaked with rain, nuzzling
    the window where it cries to come in.

The cobbler's nails spat on a bench; a
    hammer; a sole curling from his last.

A jay's feather against her cheek –
    something borrowed, something blue –

she waits under trees for the cobbler boy.
    A cartwheel slips away from the forge

slurring its drunken downhill speech, its iron
    consonants cursing to the river bridge.

There sinks the smith's band, wheelwright's
    measure, the spoke-shave's chaff of elm.

Grass stains the boy's shirt. A shot cracks in
    the wood. He bites her throat and enters.

If bad drains didn't kill them, it was gin, colonial
    wars, old age pulling their teeth and bones.

We're working late tonight, remembering things
    beyond these scrolls of virtuality, then

glancing up to see our faces specked by rain
    inside the darkened window's VDU.

And that other time – that sheen of green,
    ramsons stinking on the boy's fingers

the girl's pleasure purring in her throat,
 his seed washed from leaves like

melting pearls; drizzle falling, voices way-
 off, her nails scoring his arm.

What next? The cat blinking, the river
 rising over the wheel, the men

staring at the flood, its tea-coloured stain
 of peat, its current toiling to pull

the village to itself, stone by stone
 from where their fathers lifted it.

NARCOLEPSY

Old men go narcoleptic anywhere but bed;
        they spend the day spark-out in chairs sawing
through a dream, french-kissing death.
        They stop breathing, then wake, sad, suspicious
and surprised in a life that seems so new,
        urgent and strange; a world filled with stares
of grandchildren, insistent questions, the impatient
        shades of wives and workmates. They
reach for denials, beta-blockers, disclaimers;
        they clutch Zimmer frames, hearing aids, amulets;
a glass of ginseng cordial, brandy, hemlock or
        creme de menthe, puzzled by voguish customs,
outlandish uniforms, insignia, escutcheons,
        gadgets, currencies or slang. They wake to
ruched coffin lids, the thud of soil, the pursed
        lips of surgeons, their pulse's rope of light flicking
on a malachite sea. They hover like humming
        birds over the faded shimmer of their selves.
Old men slumber over dinner, mid-breakfast or
        sentence; they doze in shareholders' meetings,
surf the unelected chambers of democracies,
        nod off at masonic rituals, executions, christenings,
baptisms, the burial of friends they hold a grudge
        to still. They wake without guilt, slewing mugs of
tea, champagne flutes, gold watches, goblets of
        blood, pieces of a jigsaw puzzle of the world.
They endorse new penalties, level scores, rack
        up a feud, exact revenge. They wake in tepid water
to their daughters knocking at the bathroom door,
        the knowing smiles of *aides de camp*, the mad
stare of assassins they'll coolly offer an aperitif;
        they wake snuffling their truffle of a prostate to
loosen shoes, garters, bow ties and collar studs,
        coming-to in motels, Cadillacs, brothels, on bidets,
in hamlets, townships and tenements, tetchy,
        tenebrous and tired. Nocturnal, they lap at sleep's
blue milk, mooch empty rooms, push bells to

rouse dead servants from eternal sleep. They
prowl the levels of the house, half-blind,
        undentured, stumble-footed but sure in the
memory of newel post and stair. They pour
        libations to the dust, watch old movies, wash
in silver light, tidy the kitchen, mop a floor, sift
        wedding albums, watch a snowstorm gather or
rain strike glass which shows them suddenly old
        beyond the night. They hail insomniac brethren:
pavement artists, sleep walkers, rapists, burglars
        breaking forlorn mirrors of the street. They attend
to heating pipes, a radio's Esperanto of static,
        discern dawn's ember beyond an estuary, see
men bundled into cars, their gestures, their cries
        of innocence. Then back to the roofscape with
its gossip of smoke and solitude, its pigeon shit
        and skein of sodium lights that insulates the dark.
Briefly comatose, they do the swastika on dance
        floors, waltz lovers in black frocks to immolated
death-camp orchestras. They recall faces without
        names, journeys lost from destinations, schedules
without date or detail; they fight duels with sabres
        or chased pistols, plot *coups d'états*, adultery,
or worse. They clock-on at office, foundry or
        lathe, relax at the rudder of a ketch, ride bare-
back, paraglide, finesse protocol, bribe guards,
        choose noble exile over death, somnambulate
the glittering fable of their past. They elude us,
        born again to the Beyond, unredeemed, in hock
to nullities. Hush now. One tick of sound could
        wake them, indigo-lipped, indignant from
discourse with the dead, from lonesome galaxies,
        the blotted ink of interstellar space. One word
returns them as amiable gods, smiling, carelessly
        ancient, their breath blowing a spun glass of stars
                against the cold.

47

ROCKING STONE

You return to the wood: its fragile understanding
of larches on limestone, wind-lick hollows, moss
pads, hart's tongue, ash plants setting in cracks,
their buds already fire-hard spears.

April light is somehow green and gold: old
chablis tilted in a glass. The edges of the world
are gone, like the time an owl flew out and you
found that great stone balanced in a gryke.

You straddled it, balanced on its stern, straddled
and rocked, until its boom sounded stone on stone
on stone. Trees flickered by and ferns and scrappy
sky, all the wood's tenuous life and yours.

Years back, that. Today, you can't find it; one
stone much like another. You guess this journey has
another meaning: loss, misplacement, not finding
what you're looking for in the winding of the day.

But that memory burns, itches on your skin: the
owl's unruffled curiosity and muffled wings, the girl's
eyes, green and bold where she swayed in her
jeans and youth and loose plaid shirt.

The way she leaned close when the stone
slanted and rocked; its age of stone under a
sea's dead tides; its boom losing you all the way
back to the curdled star-mess of creation.

You never kissed, though you could have grazed
her mouth, her neat boy's neck. This time you climb
the gate and fall, slip on humped stones, their
narwhal gleam rising through fern and moss.

Green stains your hand. Sun's coin slips into the
hills' slot. Day turns. Stumble now. Keep walking in
your wet shoes home. Tread eyebright smothered
in the grass; night comes to catch you out alone.

RAVENS AT RED BANK

a foursquare gliding dance
    a half-quadrille
an airborne masque of rare
    funereal etiquette
on the polished floor of sky
    where black is *de rigueur*

their cries bump and grate
    iron gourds from
which the lake's bright lead
    or liquid slate is poured

feathered spokes
    of a sky-wheel turning
then tumbling to a dare
    shot dead
until their wings flick out
    to flirt a carbon-
diamond sex appeal

    we stumble to a halt
stand staring
    skyward
in the wet sap-scent
    of this logged space

one birch goes up
    straight as a radio mast
its budding tines capture
    the quadraphonic sky-dance
bring it down
    to wood anemones
herb paris humble
    in the grass
the broken yokes
    of celandines

your raptured
    upturned face.

LOST VOICE

A summer cold started it; that small
    denial became a hoarse croak of
abnegation, abrogation, surrender
    or worse; it slipped from my throat –
a hand from a glove, perseverance
    from work, a coin from a purse, a tongue
from all the world's *langue* and *parole*,
    a ghost flitted from a haunting, though
it was still whole in the arched bone
    of my head, as loud as any hawker's voice
or sussurating whispers of the dead.

Silence rang like a church after mass
    or foreign boulevard at dusk or a piazza
where the tones were foreign and brash
    and the husk of a woman once beautiful
sang of loss through an open window
    from her room where a naked yellow
bulb shone for those who passed into
    darkening streets alone.

Rumours of a voice began: how it was
    out there, how it ran rippling down a long
beach hissing cadenzas of surf that fell
    back to the sea, still Cordelia-like, still
soft and low, still loyal to the king in me;
    another had it messianic, on the loose,
bawling with holy pain, clawing its way
    up a crack of schist on some Eastern
Ararat so it could preach into a
    scorched-out desert plain.

At last I heard its shy reprise, its rustle
    behind skirting boards, a banished
infestation back again, roach-hordes
    or the bustle of mice signalling their
return; a phantom pain that burns even

      when the limb has vanished or tongue
is pulled up at the root like a verb
      banned because murder might turn
blue because of it or something we are
      or something we did in the beginning
and are now not allowed to do.

And now it's back, furtive and regal
      as a winter stoat, an ermine tongue
imperious with the old impatience
      to feed and to be fed, its hungry old
invective snagged on that ululating
      vulva in my throat, its way of
interpreting what's alive or dead or
      still delirious in my head, anticipating
what falls as ink with interruptions,
      inventions, flattery and vanity, its
poisoned fabulations and sad lies,
      its imprecations, its curses its glorious
encrustations of outpouring filth, its
      botched verses and perfumed perfidy,
its undeniable resemblance to me;
      its profligate use of breath; and
every word ejaculating joy; and
      every one a little death.

UNDER SLEEP

under a grasshopper canopy of song
   under a gnawed yellow moon
       royal palms and star needles
under slow bass lines and circling
   planes and sleeping toads under
       your closed eyes and wide arms
under your absence frequent as rains
   under a camel hair rug
       huddled like strangers
under beer and mango juice
   ant-borne cargoes of sugar
       under jacaranda and jack fruit
   a flamboyant's sailboat petals
       the night watchman's yawn
under dawn's earliest intimation
   of day under shrugged sleep
       our story untelling itself
everywhere ambient in wide
   opening space under your
       hand leaving my sleeve
that time and now over and over
   your hand leaving my sleeve
       and everything still unsaid
under the moon's pared rind
   the veranda's sleeping snakes
       and sloughed skin delicate
   as speckled curls of frost
       a narrow-eyed cat waiting
a pied crow waking to
   another killer day of life
       under sleep still splashed
on your eyelids under
   the fear that I'm forgetting you
       of all things of everything under
charcoal smoke and burned
   hide and fried goat and Nile
       perch and tilapia and kerosene

under the sky's faint whey
   of curdled blue under blood
      in the moon's sac under the
  grasshoppers again their
     psalm's ecumenical silence
under the dawn and the day
  before we know it waking
     from each other pearled
  with distance with desire's
     fabulous soaking dew.

EUCALYPTUS

The night-light shivers, sweats
vapour, flickers to our
childhood fevers.

Its flame rides liquid wax the way
a mariner's compass needle
floats on mercury.

We lie still, breathe incense, feel
the room's mural of shadows
soft as ibis feathers.

I love the smell of Eucalyptus
you say, your parched palm
almost burning mine.

We go like dead pharaohs in our
barque of a bed, sails full of a
desert's funerary breath.

Camels gaze calmly, the Nile's
waters rise and whisper near
enough to trail a hand.

That's an owl calling from the elm
that lightning broke; unlucky
in all this African dark.

The night's a jackal lapping stars
from our window; its studded
tongue curls around us.

I stare out, think of continental drift,
the Earth's plates sailing apart,
the way we've circled each

other all our lives like a planet
and its moon, and not known
which was which, even

before we met, fell sick together
or lit this flame in our temple
of unknowing

how we became or why or
where we'll navigate
tonight.

FRENCH HEAT

It's the rasp of meat flies as you drink from
    your hands in a long kitchen, the
flat-pressed wheat fields machined to
    gold braid, the memory of Gitanes, anise
clouding, the village square a-scream
    with swifts; it's the scrubby edge of town,
the sub-station humming, a single-track
    railway buckling into haze, a hen harrier
sleuthing her shadow across straw
    bales; the moist shadows of the house,
the limp heads of dog roses, your
    moustache of sweat, your throat's
glistening rivulet; it's the trees of
    the forest straining, a million green verbs
failing to express themselves, the
    pressure of water in trunk, capillary and
leaf, transpiration the sun drives into
    darkly shimmering columns that lightning
breaks to white-smoking pulp at night;
    it's the wood wasp hovering ancient and
alert, a brown moth folded in a towel,
    the creak of roof tiles over purlins, your
nipple magnificently out of scale, your
    breast a piste of cream above my eye,
your shoulders tanned against pillows
    and something circling afternoon's mauve
chimera of trees, spiraling outwards,
    transcendent, its utterance pure and
        untranslatable.

A COUNTRY ON FIRE/SKY BURIAL

WORD-HOARD

Sweat of the palm darkening haft,
earth clod on the iron blade-head,
I swung a broad mattock in the graveyard,
cleared dock and nettles from old headstones,
discovering their inscriptions.

Biting into the dry crust of earth it lifted
the roof from a swarming hole –
wasps rose in a nimbus of furious wings.

Vengeful at wreck of their labour,
the sudden letting in of light,
they gave chase to my retreat,
ran fiery needles into hand and thigh.

Years later, broaching the word-hoard,
meaning half sunk to darkness,
I remembered the rising of wasps
from their golden wax-glinting comb,
sunlight penetrating darkness,
eggs exposed in their palace of sleep,
the air kindled by wings.

Then I saw the cache uncovered at last:
the first gleam of the architecture
of the tongue's long garnering,
hoarding its potency for centuries,
poised at the mouth's moist entrance.

TODMORDEN

This is the true constriction:
heart-gripping rock wringing
its folk out like rags,
the valley deep
as a deep wound
set below staring outcrops,
under interminable rain.
Mills and terraces pack together,
their bible-hearted chapel stone
breathing darkness, dripping
sleet slung from hill farms'
dilapidation where sheep blacken
between snows, drag their ragged
fleece-bundles and stare down
disappearing roads.

This is the pass through heartlands
concussed with looms and locomotives;
laundry beating on lines, old men
bent under rheumatic weather
on drenched cobblestones
where market traders yell
in smoke smudged air.

Hills gape at man's audacity
to build in their cleft,
blocking the artery
with stone
and work
and religion,
damming up its pulse
in the anguish of the machine.

Heart's worsted wears thin
in raw Pennine air,
against infernal rain
bleak upon the eye,

yet the blood's urge torments
with visions of Jerusalem,
city of jasper and emerald,
of brass bands and choirs
hailed from the mouths of chapels
from which textiles drag themselves
unrolling
beneath bulrushes,
booming
below the harebell's outcry.

EVEN OWLS ARE VOICELESS

Branded like Lucifer's blood with fire, hearts
black as the hearthstone where we lie, they
march inland from their beached craft,
inward from the bitter sea.

Aliens with a foreign tongue, ferocity that
speaks fire flies this warlike banner of speech.

Through the trembling night they toil, their
torch flame gleam on weapons, teeth, the
red beards of invaders in its lust.

Leaves shudder and turn in the passing flare,
even owls are silent in the soughing wood and
underfoot the ground treads softly as a pelt.

Their flame falters in the wind then blazes,
seeking the valley where we lie; stars send
us their pain through infinity but the wise
moon turns her face away.

Beneath our bodies the stones grow cold,
cobwebs sag and glisten under dew and
not a dog barks warning to the night.

Waking from the first sleep, I reach out, find
your smooth belly with my hand. Passion rises
between us like fear – without a word I part your
thighs and take you in the breathless dark.

The forked flame moves towards us like a tongue:
even owls are voiceless in the still woods.

A COUNTRY ON FIRE

Traveling south by night to meet you takes
me through a country on fire: all the erupting
wastelands of the north crawl past the windows
of this train. Coal and steel, the smoke-burned
sinews, stretch out down valleys where the sullen
heaps of pit-head and foundry glow their hellish redness,
reflect in canals that run smouldering by this railway
then pitch abruptly back into the scorched night.

Rotherham and Sheffield go by like holocausts,
flaming orange through the darkness as if fired
by brand-bearing Norsemen in their plunder.
Past these works with their heaps of steel
rusting beside the track, past grim wagons of coal
gleaming in sidings for the furnace to leap at
the dark chaos of fire drags its flames across country,
searing it back to the bare nerve, the pitted bone of hills.

And my own blaze for you burns as fierce
and hopeless as the ashy ruination of this land
that cannot slough off its tormenting infernos;
curses this slow-forging railroad of pain
that keeps my ingot body molten with desire
from final immersion, quick cooling of its fire.

LIMESTONE

Poised under the sun's incineration
men in white crane forward.

A dead silence.

Bowler treads his run-up,
batsman takes stern guard
and waits to make a stroke.

Each summer the village team loan this field,
mow the rough grass and mark a crease in lime;
four stone walls mark the boundaries –
beyond them hills spectate the ritual game.

Through the long afternoon
they bowl their spin and swing,
are cut or driven away, until one ball
turns in more sharply from the pitch
and headstrong batsman swipes empty air –
then a stump is taken clean out
and bails fly up towards the jubilant men.

First innings over
the beer tent is loud with talk –
hay-time and cattle prices
and weather faired up –
as the players crowd in
to cram sandwiches and ale.

Above a stunted line of trees
the hills' white shoulders glare in sun,
sculpted by ice and meltwater
millions of years ago;
after a lifetime in the same valley
the men hardly spare them a glance now,
their way of doing things
so ingrained with limestone.

Sun loses its stridency
and the game resumes.

Tree-shadows lengthen on stark slopes,
a skylark sings above mid-wicket,
hanging as if carved from stone.

The ball soars to gruff cheers
and scuffs over a wall for six
scaring a lapwing from her eggs;
hills gaze down,
veiling with slow purple,
waiting for and wanting nothing.

When the final ball is bowled
the keep squats on his haunches,
balanced for the take.
The bowler sends down a teasing leg-spinner
that curves in air an eternity
before pitching to the bat;
the players cup their hands and wait,
behind them, the centuries' shadows lengthen.

ALUM POT

This is the entrance
to the speech of water,
the exit from the cries
of birds.

Ash and hawthorn stitch
rock lips to the moor:
roots are sutures,
moss makes a green salve
on a void misted with light.

This hole is a magnet
joining bone to bone:
your agility, your warm
wind-tasting skin
to the jarring dark.

Skylarks start up from the moor,
flesh nervous white ensigns;
limestone emerges from grass –
whalebone from deep water.

Alum pot swallows itself,
never-ending breathless gulp
of its stone-hoarse larynx:
the eye's pupil finds a mirror
of black.

Hands scrabble for grip
at the spray-wet bark of trees,
the cries of gulls ricochet
from the rim of the tunnel
that has reared upright
to let light fall through
a peat beck's flung prisms.

This is the entrance
and the exit:
Alpha and Omega
of the wind-choked, sky –
dizzy, grass-bewildered
travellers who are dared to fall
into the possibilities
of their lives.

GENESIS

a statue in Seravezza marble by Jacob Epstein

I'm staring into darkness that flows through
this continent of stone; the man's chisel lids
my eyes which half open, sense light through
an opaque integument. He wakes my ears
with the chinks of this stone tomb falling.

Inside the pale globe of my belly a child
like a fish sways in the amniotic sluice
of stone; his chisel etched this life on mine,
lowered my gaze to breasts where marble
seethes with milk.

The man's eyes touch me tenderly as his
fingertips that bled to shape me from
some slumbering hillside.

He leans his shoulder to mine, attending
to my lips where words have not yet woken,
chiselling my thighs' pressure to push
against this current of stone.

The child is heavy, heavy: can it feel the
light it pushes towards with such faith?

The man smiles. His touch is a fever
I dream to cool. Oh, to soak him up in
coolness! Give him back the stillness,
the dark, the peace I stand inside.

NIGHT SHEEP

Headlamps are harvesting darkness, moorland
is swathed by light then returns to its secret
consumption of time.

Snow banks either side, sheep on the road,
their eye-crucibles emerald
in starless black.

Sheep tongues are devouring tarmac,
devouring rock-salt with oil
and tortured tyre rubber.

Sheep gathering: a thousand grass-stained tongues,
a thousand incomprehensible messages licked
from under wheels and axles.

I found a skull once, complete with horn-sheaths,
latticework of sinus perfect even after frost
and crows had dined there.

Memento Mori. Reminder of ourselves, the waiting
architecture of bone, the socket-deep
grin biting at speech.

Their breath is carbon monoxide, their fleeces the
dag-tailed leavings of furriers; tongues rasp at
crusted snow like files, rolling up their
cud of knowledge.

The road is a routeway to nothingness: it heads for
the spaces between lights, charting the deepest
channels where houses and farms are licked
from land by night's black mouth.

Tyres sluther and whine on frozen ridges, sheep
scatter in a green comet-hail, tongues close
in behind, erasing tracks; away in front
horned heads bend to their labour,
licking the labyrinth deeper.

NORMANDY

Hidden footprints tread orchards
hung with white rags of blossom.
Jackboots kissed this earth
with their black print;
cattle graze over the memory,
hawthorn flowers are lazily
shaken over old heel-wounds.

In the village there are monuments
to the soldiers of both wars;
a grey stone remembers others –
martyrs who died against trees –
gagged with torn sheets, their eyes'
petals closed by Mausers as spring
made cider through the trees' sap.

Farms lie empty from reprisals:
their red clay tiles tilt, drunk with light.
A track heads nowhere through grass
rank with buttercups, then finds a clutch
of half-crazy hens pecking for grit.

Wood pigeons glide in and out of
the sanctuary of trees, they roost
with the murmur of leaves a green
liquid in their throats;
already the high meadow is raked
for its last wisps of hay.

Soon they will clean the cider press
scraping last year's pips from crevices,
scalding the bleached oak as they
would a pig grown fat on windfalls.

The great screw glides up and down
the oiled shaft, its turning dizzy
with downward force, crushing the
wild, secret juice from history.

NEIGHBOURS

Fifteen floors high, these flats pile
family above family and hold us there
between the hunger cries of gulls:
only glass shields us from their wings,
refracts their ravenous eyes.

An acid wind ulcerates our views,
throwing pedestrians to the roads,
litter across allotments where stray
dogs shit and snarl and battle
towards the butcher's dustbins.
Cars beach themselves at shops:
their cargoes spill out over back seats
where abandoned children reach out
from their harnesses and howl.

Each night streetlamps, like
lymphocytes, engulf the stars:
televisions blare, sleepers turn,
the neurotic flares of music
burning their blood to ash.

Each morning we leave our rooms
afraid to meet silences that prowl
the empty falling flight of stairs.

We pack the elevator's black walls:
its hoarding of glass gives us back
our faces like something hunted.
Only our shoulders touch, not our
eyes which search the floor for
swallowed cries, evidence of lives
that hurtle the long shaft.

THE DISAPPEARED

El Salvador

He has disappeared into the picture.
His mother holds it against her womb and we scan it:
there is no blood, the boy is not manacled,
not lying in the sweet grass of a clearing
being brutally beaten, his fingers not
broken because he plays the guitar and sings.
He does not sing, he has no guitar, he has no fingers:
he has a stiff suit and a newly married face.

It is the boy's birthday; a bag of sweets
lies in the sticky sun on his school bench.
The children sing *Happy Birthday* in Spanish
whilst he cries helplessly, scuffing his toes in dust.
His mother washes shirts at the stream
smacking them on the hot concrete slabs.
She smiles, hearing his song rise into the air
then fall among the throbbing grasshoppers.

An army jeep goes through the village.
It stops. A soldier who has not shaved rips
down a poster with a man's face on it:
the man still smiles with his torn face.
The boy is watching from the adobe church:
he sees the black priest run from house to house,
he sees plastic flowers spill over the graves.

The boy's mother suspects him:
some currants have gone missing.
She clucks his name – *Philippe, Philippe* –
he drops the fistful in her lap and escapes.

The boy lies awake thinking of the fireworks
tomorrow; in the next room one of the workers
from the new road is talking with his mother.
The man is called Carlo. Once he gave
the boy a dollar just to go away.

His mother's face has sunk like a rock under
the grey suds of the stream; he cannot bring
it back unless he presses his forehead hard
against the wire cage.

A van with no windows arrives out of
the sunshine. The driver leans from
his cab, jerks a thumb backwards.

Somewhere, out of view, a man is
laughing; the fat guard is laughing.

GRINTON MINES

Sheep are the eternal warriors: their horned
war-hoods holding down the horizons, their
boney foreheads butting at a grey cloud –
mass vague as their cognition.

Water spills down from old workings,
lead mines worm through the hill,
burrowing from dale to dale:
one time a man, belly down,
could worry through like a fluke.

Smelthouse and peat store are slowly
falling, emptied of heat, vapours, sweat.
The long flue on the hillside has
coughed up its last smoke: it
staggers, stone by stone into peat.

All the evidence is in the stone:
Sea lilies, coral, brachiopods,
the lost life forms evolving towards
this moment, plundered by toiling men
inside earth's galena-rich gut, their drill-
scarred fossils blasted towards daylight.

No one piece fits another: white
chert, black chert, limestone,
gritstone; their edges ragged,
our fingers touching, running
over the cusp as if we held
a broken moon.

Then rain comes, a slamming
black tonnage of sky and we are
running to shelter in the hollow
of the cold hearths, our hearts
running together like ore.

Our numbed faces touch,
our kiss is wet with rain.

Grouse warn with their harsh laughter:
they whirr from the moor, a sudden
demonic volley scattering into mist,
into the future that stands somewhere
beyond our eyes.

SKY BURIAL

above Crummackdale

Nothing here but stone,
white stone with its aborted flesh,
its vertebrae gnawed by wind,
bleached bone.

Six black mares to carry me:
their hooves and the hearse tyres
shod in iron to dint the earth
under that last hawthorn tree.

Then four friends to bear me high
into the limestone scars:
stretcher me up or let me walk
half-dead yet full of peace, to lie

between these rocks like a sun-struck hare;
over me my eyes will pull a sky picked clean,
thorn trees' stooped shadows slanting east,
the leafless season, stark and bare.

Tie my silk scarves to cairn stones
for wind to tatter their last good-byes,
as if I still strode into gathering storms
where I learned to love to be alone.

They'll mount a fierce assault upon my eyes,
those ravens in that valley; that way
I won't be afraid of darkness, of lies
that lead us, lightless, into empty skies.

Enough mourners to file singly over scree –
but they'll wear headphones and, coming through,
wild jazz to make them breast the fell
and feel the soul inside me bursting free.

Then leave me, telling no one that I'm here
and no one will come; leave me
dead or dying with my thoughts –
black swans landing on a windless mere.

I'll drink the emptiness of rain, sky, rock,
lie in ferns and harts-tongue
with my own tongue stilled, bridled
for ravens' cries to mock.

And if I meet other skalds with battered lyres
I'll play them Bird and Coltrane
until their eyes ignite
and Valhalla jives in mead-fed fires.

Unhitch the hearse then head for town,
some bar where I got drunk on bitter ale.
Above all, don't cry; don't cry but live
and leave me for the sky to own.

MORECAMBE BAY

Our feet crush the coracles of shells;
mud-flats deepen from the sea wall,
planed by a tide's dragging brown blade.
Oyster catchers spoon shingle, the grey
ash of knot and sanderling flakes up
into sky crackling with their cries
and joint-racking cold.

An old man watches wintering curlew:
his overcoat is tied with string, his
dog investigates a scummy tidemark.
A couple walk hand in hand at the sea's edge:
sun warps their shadows onto sand, wind
nudges them towards the feeding birds.

A fishing boat slowly trawls the lamination
of light upon water; our feet soak in
limpet-struck pools; your scarf streams
scarlet from dark tangles of hair that
tonight will taste of salt.

The cranes at Barrow-in-Furness break
the skyline with iron exclamations;
rivers lug their silt out to sea, weighted
with excrement and isotopes.

Wind x-rays our hands. The bones
show clean as fillets. Mud sucks
at our feet, lets go, sucks, sucks.

CLIMBING AT HEPTONSTALL QUARRY

The will of the spidering men
has split the rock:
gritstone sweats out their palm-grease
the sun clambers over a grey arête of cloud.

Water globules seep from the cracks,
wobble past their sweating shoulders to
smash on jackdaw-shit debris below.

These men are climbing into the rock,
jamming themselves into honey-coloured, warm,
unleavened stone with groaning insteps.

Their minds have gone dark,
narrowed by sheer upward motion.

Rock surform elbows, knuckles, fingertips:
all around golden faces have sheared off,
clean and empty.

The future has no finger holds
yet the men rise upwards, upwards, upwards
into the lip of the overhang
into the shadows that grip their hands and pull.

CROW SQUADRON

The sun they flew out of plays
with blacks and blues
in their tattered plumage;
they hang in formation as if they
flew into barbed wire and broke
their wings over its steel barbs:
their necks tilt, pointing
their bills at the stake,
at lost targets below.

Flies have blitzed their eyes
yet their calls – blind
radio-operators – still spiral
in the dazed, hot air above woods.

The gamekeeper's imperatives
came smoking from the muzzle of his gun
without afterthought:
one moment circling the earth's map,
the next blasted sideways,
twisting and falling
into the blurred land.

Their claws still clench this sudden mystery,
their eyes' sockets peer
into the skull's turret:
gunner and navigator
have flown their last mission,
bluebottles lunch
on last-minute miscalculations
and the bone struts shine.

Above an airstrip of tree-tips,
from the twin hangers of a rookery,
formations float up
into the quickening currents:
their cries search the sky,

the earth,
daylight's retina;
their hunger pinpoints
crash-landings from which
the warm lives will spill.

They see the man moving as dust
upon their eyes' screen:
only his gun is immortal.

SNOW FROM THE NORTH

SNOW FROM THE NORTH

Tonight snow comes squalling from the north:
it curfews streets to silence,
smothers footsteps, car tyres, voices
from the golden doorways of pubs.

Driving into flickering ice-flames,
rooftops are preened with cold's plumage;
headlights glance on white wings
that beat in steady sweeps of snow.

The road dips and turns, brakes slew the car
into invisible bends, tyres lurch
as it climbs in an agonising gear
onto a hilltop where drifts bury the moor.

Below, lines of yellow lights waft out,
wind spins its flakes over Burnley;
the town falls asleep, house by house,
surrendering to the white bird's dreams.

Dead trees lean out from the dark,
headlights amaze their eyeless staring;
their lost souls clamour in the wiper blades,
hiss under the tyres' treachery.

Only my hands between this and me:
they poke out from the grey cuffs of my coat,
wrenching the car away where it swerves
towards oblivion.

I'm home, those wings still kissing my face:
up behind that window she's sleeping, not knowing
I'm here at last – still breathing, still holding
my breath – as snow lets that first star through.

AMNESIAC

The mirror shows me a map of skin
without reference points:
I have seen other men like him
and that faint scar on his temple
means nothing.

The light behind me is as clean
as the future:
whatever past I've had is splintered
like a looking glass.

I'm like a baby just born:
no worries, no shame or regrets,
no guilt about the things I've done.
The women I've loved have let me
start again; I won't miss them or wet
my pillow with bitter tears.

Yesterday, I searched my body inch by inch:
no tattoos or birthmarks, it meant nothing,
like the body of any fifty-year-old man.
My lungs tell me I've never smoked
and my heart is steady as a clock.

I stare at my hands, try to recall
what they have touched, mended, broken.
My signature may have sealed contracts,
warrants, treaties between nations;
I take a pen, fill a blank sheet with names,
accuse myself of them, one by one.

I have this vocabulary in place,
this way of speaking
which comes from nowhere.
They tell me that friends and family
will be looking for me:
it is only a matter of time.

Whatever is lost may be found.

But when I saw that man in the dock
trying to hand back his name –
flashbacks to mass graves flickering
white faces behind barbed wire – and
witnesses accusing him across forty years,
I folded the sheet, found a clean envelope,
posted it with no address.

PHOTOGRAPHIC MEMORY

The footpath trails on beyond her
into the brightest day;
just a grey trace of cloud,
stray leaves on the grass, though
it is early for them to fall.
The dog is blurred, like a genie
metamorphosing into solid air.
She stands: a hand on the fence,
a hand on the walking stick,
her cheeks bitten by wind,
rinds of mud peeling from her shoes.

I remember the holiday, not this place:
all week the sea was high and grey,
gulping our footprints from the beach.
A tea-room somewhere?
Apple or pear trees behind,
the cups thin and white as bone.
A check tablecloth, cores, crumbs.
The light is good, the shadows strong:
her feet are clutched by them, they
eclipse her eyes like burnt moons
and she is smiling.

This light is too bright, coming from
the wrong direction.
Propped up in bed, it takes away her face,
melts it into the white day outside net curtains.
Wisps of hair, everything misty,
an open book across her legs.
The clock stopped at 2.15, though
it ticked on over the hour and years.
A sixtieth of a second, f2.8 – no depth –
and blurred, the whole thing blurred,
as if my hand shook.

NIGHT RIDE

BMW R/80

The road flicks away into the dark.
bend after bend coming at him,
the headlight of the bike bobbing
on stone walls sheer as cliffs.

Young rabbits struggle to the verge,
its glare tarring their feet to the road,
dazing their fear, the engine's rage
overwhelming their thin hearts.

The white house had shaken in his mirrors,
its pale cloud drifting away. She had stood
by the window, drenched in his anger,
watching his tail light dissolve into the dark.

Pistons hurtle in their scalding oil,
horizontally opposed, but the camshaft turns
and the wheels turn and the stars are at work
like jewels in a slowing clock.

Wind tugs at his scarf
blurs everything with tears:
the speedo, the rev counter,
white lines suturing the road.

His lungs struggle against wild
buffets of air,
his heart's valves tick
into the last seconds of his will.

DROWNING AT POUZAUGES

The tip of his rod touched water,
plucking it into quick dimples of light;
sun baked the clay roofs of the town
where it dozed on the hill
under the ruined chateau
under thudding afternoon heat
that drove the dull blood in his head.

There were damsel flies haunting
the water, dogs sniffing at his heels,
no clouds, and the far cries of swimmers
on the lake's far edge chasing
invisible fish his way.

His finger nails were puttied white
with another morning's dough –
baguettes, ficelles, croissants –
his hands formed them easy as sleep
moulded dreams of the green lake's
carp exhaling pure water.

He moves a few yards down the bank,
flicking a float and baited hook onto
his own shadow that swayed and wobbled
and eddied sideways as the waters shifted.
Tonight a full moon would cast itself
upon this pale face: he would rise early
to see it wane in the valley's mist
as if it never had been real.

He felt the pull of it, the desire of it
drawing him from his sleeping wife,
from the laundered sheets of their bed
to his work at the oven behind their shop.

Poplars and vineyards were sketched green
by an unsteady, heat-stricken hand;

the horizon's melting with sky was white-hot,
hazing hour after hour into this late noon.

No sweat would cool his parched skin or soothe
the burns branding his wrists and arms.

His eyes sank into a green iris of water,
he heard a rat plop into the reeds,
the hearts of fish pulsing,
pumping their cold blood;
he heard the water sighing far-off words,
meaningless as days that followed days.

No one saw his fall, but saw water-rings
where a fisherman had been:
he did not rise to gulp a snatch of air
nor squander last breath in cries for help.
No past life flashed before his eyes –
but a peace like emeralds, discovering
the lake's lost treasure of sleep.

MOTHER AND SON

All those months, trying to get out:
a word in a shut mouth, clenched
into silence.

Only her booming heart
and the swaying dark pushing
at the bone lid of her womb.

Now she is trying to escape
into old age.

I won't let her go – she'd fly like
a sparrow through the bars of my ribs
stop to touch this cracked one,
or not fly, or sing, caged in me –

her face going back behind the caul,
her white hair drifting like smoke.

FROST

Last night a thin blade of moon,
stars pricking the blackness
of time between each other.
This morning, frost-crystallised grass,
a bronze swarf of leaves turning
and dropping from the trees,
a big sun splintering light,
shattering a still world of glass.

One magpie flies over the bus stop
where our three sons stand
stamping like small ponies
panting dragon statues
of twisting breath.
A car exhaust smokes like battle
through which they smile
and call out to me chinking
towards them from the Post Office
my pockets full of change
my hands warming the nickel moons.

This morning you went without a word:
I watched from the window
wanting this dumbness
wanting to call you back.
You drove off through falling
yellow poplar leaves
Into cold air, sun, time,
into the distance between us:
frost on the roof of the car,
frost on our tongues,
a dawning sun molten above trees.

MOLE TOTEM

They jerk on the wire,
death's agony bitten
between heavy-duty jaws.

Their paws still swim through
earth-dark, bone flippers
poised for each stroke.

Backs convulse against wind,
rain washes strychnine
through their leaky spines.

They snapped like high wires:
the lives that tiptoed fell
into the seasons' oblivion.

Moleskin dries over ribs' white
basketwork, the brown husks sway:
airborne seeds of a subterranean will.

One by one they fall, softened
by April rain, quicken, plunge
blindly back into waves of soil.

PASSING OUT

A line of swallows on the line outside;
between them on the table, breakfast plates,
a blue telegram meagre with words
as with regrets.

They tried to picture the place where he
had died: a hot country with sand and flies,
undrinkable water, beggar children, sores
on their legs, mosquitos drinking from
the corners of their eyes.

She pushed back a strand of hair,
wondering if he had thought of them;
he watched the clock from habit,
watched the door. The company would
dock his pay, his lathe stilled, coils
of bronze spilling to the workshop floor.

She could not speak, but put the kettle on:
water's tattoo rolled brittle as a drum.
They saw swallows shift and rise, pulled
airwards by their invisible urgency
to be gone.

The telephone rang, a reporter from
the newspaper had heard: could they
confirm? Could she call to do a story
on their son?

Stalled in the spotlight of his death
they agreed. She fetched the family
album and they sifted through, seeing
him grow taller on each page: from
Chaplin in the school charade to
squaddie at his passing-out parade.
And they were lost again in pride
that killed their rage.

ON CATON ROAD

The road's black skin glistened,
sloughing dawn's glimmer of light;
the motorcycle coughed, shuddered,
panted white smoke, poisoned a morning
frosted in drifts of powdered glass.

Dark silver clouds blew over;
mist hushing the river to the sea.
cold air that blasted you,
seconds ahead,
stung my eyes with ice, paralyzed
these hands where they steered the bike,
numbed my clenched mouth with speed.

Then, suddenly, your blue Suzuki
crumpled in the road,
half-darkness, a line of cars
blinking down the diversion,
people running for help.
but you lying alone –
as if you'd sinned – broken
with your unbatheable wound,
one hand held out, an oil stain
bleeding around you.

I knelt on frozen tarmac, feeling
for a pulse, pulling up an eyelid
to see your pupil narrow at the light.
It stared back: wide, empty, black.

A woman's coat laid over you
where you lay across white lines.
Headlamps veiled by fumes
wept light over us:
mine still burning,
yours smashed in the road.

My breath blossoming to steam,
yours a crushed flower petalled
in your chest, unfurled fingers
curling slowly, the car that killed you
clucking as it cooled.

I loosened your helmet, pulled
the scarf from your dumb mouth;
your blood smearing my hands,
your thin wrist signaling nothing, as
if my premonition had cheated you of life,
kneeling amongst crazed lights, your
knuckles' white dice spilled from my hand.

When the ambulance came they lifted you in:
a fatality whose wallet would hold all the clues.
I turned for home, steered
towards the locked house of tomorrow
for which there is no key.

Dawn melted through blazing clouds,
throwing my shadow on the verge:
carburetors breathing cold clear air,
tailpipes hoarse with lust for the road,
the police already searching for your name.
And me, with your dead eyes in mine,
speeding away through a brilliant morning.

CLIMBING WITH A DEAD MAN

The day he fell his cry grabbed at sky,
his body's dark star wheeled the void:
I held him, belayed, took the strain,
until he climbed back past me, spewing blood.

At every hold his eyes dulled with hate,
at every rest he coiled the rope's long
hiss, betrayed to rock that bears us, that
licks us with a black parched tongue.

This morning we woke on the totem of the
crag: it rears dumbly, fractured, bare. Later,
sun will pinion moves across its sleep,
our fingers sweating on its dreams of air.

He makes the moves, and I follow, nudged
by thermals, testing each flake. Questions
piton deep into my stone-numb, fissured
mind: it is days since he spoke.

I climb his chimneys slippery with blood,
lodge my feet on red stains leaked from his
toes: he takes the rope but does not see,
his eyes torn out by screaming hawks.

The night of the day he fell I dreamed
of rain lashing rock, blue ropes ablaze
with lightning, St. Elmo's fire spidering
between us on the drenched face.

But his shoulders were heaving towards
some hold in that hurricane of night, hands
bearing down to raise his body to a ledge,
balanced on a flickering crux of light.

Now a raven comes close to watch us,
its wing-tips scattering clouds' white
spores: it rides their solidity like waves,
its eye sees life leaking from our pores.

I have forgotten how many days we have
climbed, his empty eyes are blind to time:
I say that we are hands on a clock-face of rock,
his purple tongue lolls and I bite mine.

He takes the rope, I gasp for it, face grazed
against the sharkskin rock; sun falls back
behind its splintered spines - each night
he chooses the ledge to bivouac.

No sleep: canvas flaps with moans of the dead
who cling to this stone needle without hope.
At dawn I ask him if he has heard their cries –
he shakes his eyeless head and coils the rope.

He makes the moves and I follow, he gives
me rope, I take it tasting fear. The rock
twins us, hold by hold: I see myself,
the void, steps reaching into endless air.

AN IRISH BISHOP IN PERU

He watches soldiers goose-step in the square:
Huancavelica's public prosecutor, a pair
of army generals close behind.
Each soldier's face a red-black rind
of camouflage paint, though it's not yet night
and there is nothing to hide from but the light.

At his house a letter sealed from Rome warns
him to be circumspect whilst one from home
tells of cold Antrim rain and labour on the farms.
Soldiers' boots crash, shouldering arms they
climb into the truck; a British camera crew are there
to capture peasant faces blanked out by despair.

The journalists came to see him, played their tape.
It catalogues the Disappeared, death, torture, rape.
Angel Escobar Jurado's gone: his wife cries
out for justice, hearing official lies
nail down the certainty that he is dead:
no resurrections granted, but *Te Deums* of lead.

A man in hiding tells haltingly through tears
how they trussed, hung, martyred him for days.
This woman shows how soldiers bowed her head:
a communicant three point-blank bullets left for dead.
'Of course here have been excesses, they will pass.
Some of the soldiers come to celebrate my mass.'

Helicopters darken sky, a swarm ordained
to break these whispering huddles as they form.
The bishop turns to go, knowing it's too late when
droughts of faith are slaked by sacraments of hate.
Too late to dream of Ireland, write his learned tome,
too late to break the silence spreading out from Rome.

Soldiers' eyes are stones behind their rifle stocks;
the tongues of priests have grown as still as rocks.

HOME IN APRIL

Home is empty:
guitars are asleep in black cases,
the ashen fires smell of soot.

Silverfish shiver in the hearths,
letters pile up against the door
like snow.

Children's voices have blown away
to the broken poplar tree; their
footsteps pour down the empty street.

The telephone rings, its voices
penned – dammed souls
behind the shrill bell.

Under aching rafters generations
of the dead rub shoulders;
woodworm rock in their oak hammocks

window glass thins against Yorkshire air,
the moon's face presses in upon
a house sighing with empty beds.

Hills are tarnished with silver cloud;
the farmer, his coat tied with string, drives
up the lane towards lambs dazed with life.

A MERCENARY SOLDIER TURNS FOR HOME

I remember a line of blue hills
glimpsed through sweat - always
a day's march away - hauling the guns
towards their mirage, kites circling,
grass whispering against our knees.

A night our fires died under stars
scattered by frost, the yelps of dogs.
I stood sentry, braced against cold,
counting winters camped under freezing easterlies,
a narrow-eyed people for neighbours.

In spring we burned their villages,
took their cloth for our women, sabred
theirs as they ran into the fields
from our lust: no other woman after
ever yielded the wild taste of their fear.

Then the years quickening, weariness,
each campaign sickening like plague
in our veins, wanting each thaw, each truce
to wash us home with the wind at our backs,
out youth quenched now like a thirst.

We came back one by one, meeting the blue
lake of emptiness in the other's eyes,
knowing what they had looked at.
The old men we would become had the same stare,
gazing out to horizons brimming with cloud.

Rich men, we took wives, bred sons,
taught them war games in the dust
of the threshing floor; we told stories
haltingly, our hands flailing meaning
from the gaps between words.

Each spring I watch for my boys to come:
Ice floes break and float downstream,
wind stirs grass, an ash of memories.
No speeches return, but the face of one woman
from a forgotten war, white and still amongst the corn.

AN EEL AT LAKE CONISTON

The night sky blowing westwards,
a quarter moon silvering those star-
swallowing shoals of cloud.

Scents of wet grass bruise underfoot,
sheep bleat across meadows, whispers
smoke from our frozen mouths.

The lake is glimpsed through willows,
lights of the drowned town lapping
on its pewter gleam.

We find the jetty, walk out, lie
down to smell the rot of timber
that sways beneath us as we breathe.

Our torches light up liquid glass
dense with water mites; they
flicker in a sudden electric dawn,
swimming unafraid in its ecstasy.

Then I see it, turning above the gleam
of snagged fishing line, a torque
coiling and uncoiling, an eel, greenish,
finned like a fish but flowing landwards.

From the Sargasso, too deep for nets
or lights, it has swum here to rise
at this instant, its eyes lamping
the reeds for prey.

A rumour, a warning,
a premonition destined
at the water's broken rim.

You didn't see it, deny it, yet
want it to slide into the light:
our torch beams search this cold crucible
where I know it moves under us.

Invisible under the town's reflection,
choosing its element, shy of its own legend
it moves, beautiful as we are now – beautiful
and fierce with hope under this torn sky.

CIRCULAR BREATHING

IMAGINING THE WOODS AT KATYN

Rain is in my hair, it is bending
back leaves where the pale mouths
of convolvulus implore a silence.

A finger-bone lies at my feet,
its fine nib glistening in the rain,
writing and re-writing the same story.

I've brought a white handkerchief,
empty pockets, the clay of another
country smothering my boots to

this place where God forgot himself
again, closing his eyes so that
the rain would not fill them.

The woods tease my ears with brotherly
whispers of comfort; there is a stink
of leaf-mould and sour uniforms.

A collared dove follows her cry into
this silence, pecking at young
mushrooms which glow like skin in

the clearing where they knelt,
hands snared in prayer,
the pistol barking at their necks.

Spiders tie their gauzes everywhere:
over the iridescence of tyre-ruts.
onto leaves that shiver still.

Rain is in my hair and I am tangled
in its blue veils, stumbling across
the forest's unmerciful frontiers of light.

TODAY

Today the fields steam-up a bleating sunrise;
lambs are picky-toed on their heat.

A ginger cat strolls over rooftops
filching nestlings from the chimney pots;
her tail stiffens to an electric rod
of fur at the jackdaws' hiss.

The first swallows perch shoulder to shoulder,
divining insects that swarm below the wire;
their throats swell in lipstick kisses.
A man free-wheels home his brother's bike

his widow watching from the lattice
where clematis trails; spokes mill the light
into cruelties of remembrance, spanners jostle
in the saddle bag and the chain is hoarse.

A car starts first time, coughing politely,
smug in its blessed miracle of parts –
one virtuous life in a sinful congregation
of blown head-gaskets and exhausts.

The newscaster's voice updates us:
the situation in Ecuador, then Janáček;
his violins are urgent as sparrows
soaring in a giddy flock of notes.

That vapour trail scribes its curve
from a silver compass-point;
it wavers, gives up measuring,
then skids into ski-tracks of smoke.

There's the cat again, licking its paws,
shivering from the bloody taste of soot;
there's the glint of coffee in these cups,
sanpaku, that sudden mooning of an eye.

There's a blue vein crossing your hand,
the pulse of moment passing into moment,
there's Ecuador, Janáček, that sunburst
gasping across a wall as the clouds spill.

GIRL AT LONG LANE

The track slots into the hills' vee,
white with dust and the white hope
of leaving.

Grass tears under the teeth of sheep;
her shoes click on the path, polishing
its flat stones.

A cuckoo suckles the wood's
green air; she counts each quaver,
steps into the day's light.

Thistles spike the garden;
at dusk they bloom with moths,
with pale wing-beats.

Last night the wine of her dream
was apple-scented, its slush of ice
trickling on her tongue.

Today the farmhouse sweats steam
and woodsmoke; dance-hits billow
from the radio.

She steps over hens where they cluck
in the dirt, laughs at bees drunk
again in the foxgloves.

She drops the basket from her hip,
lifts her father's shirts into the sun
and sings.

FIRST BORN

First, a song I'd never heard,
tolling through green light,
now this shell in my back's hollow
rocking me to the edge of space.

I tread moss, wool, nest-shit;
the egg draws me up then dimples
off into air's clamour of cold –
one less, one less, one less.

My little mother comes again,
squirts grub-fat under my tongue;
she gives warmth stupidly, broods
me all night, her own chick

the quick black ball of her eye
too worry-blind to question.
That scream in the air is mine
it goes out from my skinny chest

and will not stop. But she's
too small too soon, crooning
the wrong song at my back
to stuff me full of fury.

Who can know their own nature?
Hunger is what I am and thirst,
needy for lodging and heat under
a foreigner's stinking wing.

Today something changed, that voice
at the edge of things beating up
pure bubbles of blood in my throat.
This territory is ours for the taking –

I shiver where a quiver of new
feathers pricks at my skin;
soon I'll know who and why
I am. Soon we will begin.

RUNAWAY

Back at base we put the record straight,
scald our throats with sweet tea,
sweat out the relief of finding nothing
and tell it how it was.

How ice broke under us as we tiptoed
the path's brink of frozen mud, our torchlight
hewing that hut from the dark, our
breath dulling its padlock's frost.

How little there was inside:
a hemp rope, an oil can, the reek
of tar and diesel, spent cartridges,
newspapers, white rigging repairing
windows with its trembling yarn.

How cattle bellowed behind us, then
a fox yelped, how the farm's stub glowed
as wind sucked it and how we heard the echo
of that name they kept throwing at the dark.

We say how we stood listening
and how the stream would not hush
itself across the earth's curve;
how a pheasant crackled from the woods
and the sky cleared as we squinted
for satellites, bringing the Pleiades
from their fading-trick of light.

In the morning they'll let dogs sniff
at her clothes then track her.

They'll find her huddled in that nook
of larches, still breathing, dribbling
a miracle of ice from the thumb in her mouth,
only an hour from the big sleep.

Or she'll be covered with a sheet
where the flashlight sprawled her,
the forensic squad on their hands and knees
prising clues from leaf-mould and fingernails.

Right now we're in the pick-up driving home,
empty-handed, sleepless, thinking of bleak
headlines and black waters, of a figure
who might still drag herself from the trees
towards her father's litany of all
she had to stay for.

Needles jab and flicker on the dials,
measuring each stammer of wheels on a track
where headlights stun the sheep, bounce
from night's meniscus of sky, then
find the road and sweep it clean.

A QUIET BLOKE

He was a quiet bloke, retired groundsman
at the county pitch, unmarried, childless –
the way these things are measured –
but troubled by something enough one day
to take the spade from a neighbour edging
geranium beds, down him in one, then slice
off his head, methodical as digging turves.

He went home, changed his spattered shoes
then gave himself up like a crossword clue,
muttering how he'd suffered leylandii long
enough, how bowlers followed through straight
down the track, which wasn't on, how things
build up, get worse, go unremarked –
how twenty-two yards make a chain.

Detectives checking the neighbour's trees saw
how they'd stolen away the church clock;
and sure enough, they didn't find a timepiece
in the house, even checked the quiet bloke's
wrist for the white band a wristwatch leaves, found
nothing except the sinew that years of grass mowing,
seed sowing and marking out with lime had knotted.

A reporter swore the quiet bloke smiled when
the pathologist ascribed to him some knowledge
of anatomy – he meant the way the bloke had
slipped that spade between vertebrae and turkeyed
the neighbour's head – even so, it was a gory mess
that left the jury faint, one police photographer
checking out his pension dates, the press swabbing
copy from that overgrown suburban lawn.

At the trial the quiet bloke showed no remorse,
offered no defence; he waved on sight screens
when sun dazzled the courtroom, asked for a brushing
and heavy roller at recess and, when weather broke,
greeted the usher by counting overs lost through rain;
but mainly he was the quiet bloke he'd always seemed.

As he said himself that time, chilling the duty officer
with calm reserve, things build up, go unremarked;
but on receiving sentence we noticed how he seemed
to glance down at his wrist, to bite his lip, then cast
his hand in a slow circle from the dock as if remembering
something he'd practised or always meant to do.

SPIDERS

The spiders stayed awake again.

I call you and you leave the bed
to see: at work all night
wiring up the apple trees,
the windows, the angles
of the broad bean canes,
all aerialised for some broadcast
far beyond our frequencies.

Their threads gleam like fishing line
disappearing into the air's depth,
melting in the sun which has risen
again to burn off the dew, dust shadows
from under roofs, shape-shift hills
that smoulder in heaps of cooling slag.

Spiders' reproaches are everywhere:
Work! Work! Work!
each one a steeplejack welding
his steel filaments to a frame,
a tight-rope star burnishing her own
glittering steps above the night.

They know how to wait
and how to betray,
how to say nothing and lie still,
how to seem a shadow of shadows
a silence of the silence,
how to look away whilst looking on;
their eyes multiply the frail-winged
prizes of the day.

They are hidden and waiting –
everywhere –
for that first faint touch
to bring them unblinking to the light.

It comes: expected, surprising
as my mouth reaching to kiss
pale hair on your neck's curve,
sudden as your tears, stopped
on my unbuttoned sleeve.

IMPERATIVES

Rise to one whiskey glass growing
stale, the bottle horizontal
as if you'd spun it for luck,
true north or nakedness.

Discover one letter on the mat,
morning light sprawled across
its postmark, the front gate clacking
behind the postman's step.

Shave now, wince at that splinter
in your hand which only hurts
when you remember it and probe
its sliver of steel or thorn.

Gulp coffee, go to work leaving
the bed unmade, the window open,
tapping gently like Blind Pew's stick
or a stylus clocking a forgotten groove.

Now think of coming back tonight –
of breathable emptiness – then remember
how you first arrived, hoisting
her across the threshold as a joke.

Consider the irony of things
half-built – unopened tile grout,
the shower kit from B&Q, the wall
lights' bouquets of lethal wire.

Work because work numbs your mouth
like Novocain, like sleep numbs an arm
or the fuse-box numbed your hands
that time the lights went down.

Wake again tonight, hearing cats howl
at the multiple sins of sex, imagine
how chestnut trees hissing on the hill
could be tropical surf or snakes.

At breakfast find the same letter,
unopened, propped against the salt,
its invoice of hurt outstanding
and indelibly specified.

Let sunlight on the wallpaper remind
you of pageboy hair, its gloss
when she opened the fridge, humming
a tune's unfinished bridge to things.

Watch the toaster lob flaming slices
onto melamine and through the smoke observe
a blue tit hover at the window, momentarily
exotic, a suburban hummingbird.

Stare where its wings and your eyes blur,
to where the days lie down in rows
and only the joker is set aside
in their unfinished game of solitaire.

Now junk the deck and swear
you never lied.

FLYMOWING

Flymowing the lawn all summer
was hell.

I had to keep on at it
while the grass grew like fire
and she lay upstairs
with whatever it was
coming inside her; so long
since I'd touched her, I'd
forgotten how.

No matter how much you keep it
down it grows after the least
bit of rain – that June
we had a drenching and then
the sun driving it on.

It was madness – like bloody
Vietnam – and the cats wild
for the young birds all summer.

At night I dreamed of it – eternal,
slopes of green and me alone
hacking at it with just the edges
of my hands;
she'd be asleep or lying
listening to what I muttered
about grass, about two-stroke,
the pull-start stalling.

Sometimes I thought of it
inside her, hollowing her eyes,
but that shadow was the shadow
of something growing;
one night I found myself on the lawn,
groping without a moon to see by
and weeping for something lost,
there in the grass, lost.

After thirty years you don't
talk much or can't.

Each time I'd check for stones
on the newly laid bits she'd
wanted: easy to bend a blade
or jam up on a piece of stick –
everything stops then.

Flymos?

Flymos are a bastard to start.

BLACK MARKET

It's dawn and the river steams.
He waits for you by the bridge – as they
said he would – his feet gently stamping
on the snow's crust, next to the chestnut
seller, that newsvender breathing smoke.

You sidle up to him, this zek-head
in the long coat: no salute,
you greet him with one word and hear
your own language harsh in his mouth.
No names, no pack-drill.

His eyes water in their red slits,
his lashes blinking at the cold or
at poverty. He licks a stained moustache,
his tongue furtive behind the cigarette;
already his inattention cheats you.

You are wearing your good shoes, your
warm jacket quilted against the cold
as your head is quilted against the hour
by last night's drinks. At the bar you boasted
of leaving, the whole city turning under your heel.

He thumbs the white crescents of his eyes,
a rat slicks across dead nasturtiums, sleek
as the river where it goes under the parapet.
The man gestures '*follow*', his hand an exclamation,
his nails filthy with secret work.

He smells of wet wool, stale books, of dead
philosophy, of something you want or meant
to get round to in the end but never did:
he squats in your head and his name
cannot be written down or evicted, ever.

He is your blind date, waiting as you are.
You'll follow him into the city, into
basement cafes where the soup is thin and sour,
into tanyards and shop fronts where the deals
are struck – each one, someone's bad bargain.

Nothing goes as planned. One job you said,
wanting to be on a flight, counting dollars,
seeing a softly torn sea below, curving palms,
a catamaran far out and a beach-house where
cool women are sipping rum spilled over ice.

Now you've got packets hidden in the floor,
daren't answer the phone, or that late-night knock.
The landlady's eyes are black with sudden hate
and her face shows you what you are. Today
you rang a friend and the line died.

Tonight they'll hand you an address, a bridegroom's
photograph – enough to know him at close range –
something wrapped in oiled cloth, its chambers
clicking in your hand. Then used notes, half now and
half later. Then moments ticking themselves empty.

WAITING FOR O'MALLEY

My orders are to wait for O'Malley
then stiff him in any corner of this field
that's cold as a promise never kept,
foreign and windswept as a Belfast alley.

Furrows are unfreezing from the night,
curving into a dawn raw as the eyes
of sleepless squaddies, glazed with frost
and thaw and gusts of icy light.

A flock of goldfinches feeds on thistle heads,
their down glossy as a brochure of somewhere
far away. We watch the track where he will come,
imagine the path he treads.

The goldfinches stare and peck
and peck and stare like blind prophetic
birds of stone; they glean harsh oracles
of peat-water that gurgle faintly from the beck.

These co-ordinates are mapped in O'Malley's
head; he knows where the cache is, which target,
when. The sun is bitter as cordite, bright
as the copper that jackets lead.

A kestrel hovers: wing tips blur
to hold it still as it interrogates
the land for movement, searching
for indiscretions that give its retinas a kill.

Each moment of the waking day
we think of him and without hate, knowing
that he'll come stepping soon into our sights
we're anxious, as if a loved one was late.

Our fingers are stiff and frozen to the bone,
our breath is white as fusillades of river mist.
This is the kind of duty no one likes –
the kind of duty that must be done.

A RIDDLE FOR THE SERBIAN WARS

I am smoke curling from the cannon's mouth
a cockerel's white feather

I am the cry of women, the keening
shell that falls into a town's sleep

I am the roof beams burning
and the cellar's huddled dark

I am the poem in a rapist's mouth
the rictus of hanged men

I am this hushed breathing
this shrinking prayer this litany of lies

I am the speck in a neighbour's eye
that covets your thistled acre

I am a white eagle, a white dove
a white face pressed to the wire

I am the knock at your door
the torchlight checking your face

I am the soldier's unsheathed pride
the slurred song of a nation

I am the cartographer drunk on ink
my hand on the pen the trigger the pulse

I am the question glinting at the border
the black stamp across your name

I am a dumb witness a twisted tongue
a language pecked out and sung by crows

Who am I?

DUET

Today the wind is in the piano, zithering
until bichords and trichords almost hum -
the way I almost whisper you my dream,
its diminuendo of passing years.

One day the wind will sing like this
and leaves will fall into your violin
the way autumn fell on your hair
and silvered it, the way it breathed
onto your manuscripts and scrolled
them into yellow curls.

You lie under the days' mysterious light
understanding only the air, its gavotte
in the piano's polished case, its easy
ebb and flow as your wrist bows slow
notes towards life, future, or something
like it that my fingers search for.

The wind quavers in our dream of days,
this illusion of anticipation and accord
still in our heads where violin and piano
tread fine legato footsteps; downstage
we see to things beyond brocade curtains
and intent faces, things which soon we only
hear and then a tune we half remember,
fumbling for notation, key and tempo.

Even now we hardly hear it.
No applause, but my hands at your temple,
soothing it without haste or words because
the wind has dried our mouths, surprising
us with things still left to say, because
your eyelids lifting leave me reading clear
grey grace notes where I know I'll never
stop looking or hearing us begin.

STORM LARKS

Sky is black as a ciné film spooling its last
reel; imageless, burned by the light, its
white-gashed celluloid flickers overhead.

The horizons tremble, then stand still,
accepting the warm rain; our breathing falters,
uncertain as purple in the sun's fading bruise.

This frequency is all wow and flutter and rumble
on the earth's slow platter, its grindstone
flinting out split-second streaks of light.

The gleam across your face fixes it here:
white, ecstatic with shushed exclamations –
then bass notes beginning below hearing's octaves.

It's ironic we don't think of God now, only
of the ions colliding, those fronts of heated air
and copper dousing-rods drinking an electric blue.

But it's death-sky music, you said so,
your hand on mine glimpsed as a claw of bones,
so old it could be winged or scaled, half-human.

Lightning fuses air's nitrogen, cattle stumble
awash in curdled milk; ponies' eyes panic,
their mouths foaming at rain's polished bit.

The voltage goes to ground, missing the uncoiled helix
of acids that wash away, futile for a billion years
until the chance of it lights like a struck match.

We're sheltering by this gable-end, watching
the town blitzed to monochrome, seeing skylarks stall
then fly on singing into the air's stunned height.

THE DREAM OF THE CIRCUS DWARF

I crouch in sawdust and lion shit
watch the crotch of the new girl
glitter on the high wire
and chew my tongue like a dog;
the crowd fall silent, the apes
are lewd in their cage of laughter.

The lights are searching for her,
sweeping out that smoky canopy
where she has vanished and the wire
gleams, impossibly fine.

Now she shimmers from the ladder's
last rung, somersaults, takes her bow,
elusive as a trick with handkerchiefs
or a magic box or a smiling woman
sawn in half; she slaps her thigh,
passes me in this pit of shadow,
spits back their gaudy applause.

She sweats garlic, scowls often,
fucks hungrily behind the caravans,
taking a new man each night
and every one hare-lipped or limping –
even the Russian hunchback's had her.

This way, it makes her perfect.

One day she came as I threw fish
to the seals, dragged her hand
down my tattoos – the blue swan
on my wrist, the black snake
at my shoulder – put her mouth
to my back and breathed on me
as you'd breathe to polish silver
or a glass to peer through.
I dropped the bucket's dead shoal
into the pool and fled.

I am my own master:
there'll be no caressing me,
no petting of my body – she'll
tire of loose fucking first,
of losing herself in the dark gap
between guy lines and brooms,
stuffing her shirt lap in her mouth
to come shuddering and gasping
like an expert, an artist.

She's watching me take water
to the elephants; her face
is young, her nipples hard
as buttons when she brushes
against me, imploring.

She sees me reading my almanac,
marking the map of Ursa Major
with purple ink; she follows
me outside to watch what I see
beyond the awnings and the road,
beyond the stars' chart turning,
the hills' anvil beating
up dawn's smoke of cloud.

She asks me what I hear when
I put my head to the ground
and lie listening at the earth,
what I weep for when I weep
for the exile of this life -
what I might have been or am.

Tonight Mars enters Leo;
I'll sleep with that planet's
brand burning in my ribcage,
dream her high-stepping grace
through all its scarlet fogs.

I am the rod of correction
in her hands: pliant, slim
as a stoat's whisker, quivering
in the hushed trembling
of her steps upon the wire.

Their faces are upturned to
watch us, dim and rapturous;
her eyes level me at the horizon
where it spins below the night;
she flexes her thighs, squeezes
damp palms, pulls in her belly,
steps out to where only I can
keep her from the space
hollowed by that fuming light.

FOX

The fox in the headlights
knows it shouldn't be here,
caught on the road through
the larch wood, just stepping
out to the chicken coop.

The fox is skittish;
it's made a *faux pas*,
executes a sorry jump
from pointed toes – a ginger
novice in the dancing class.

This is a thin fox caught
in sharp light, nervously
swishing the white tip
of its tail, painting itself
out into the dark.

A few strokes and it's gone
into a chiaroscuro dusk;
it shouldn't have been there
on the road, in this poem –
dancing, up to no good.

NEIGHBOUR

Today a man comes knocking at your door,
his laughing face is hidden in his hand,
his pale eyes shift like eyes of sand.

Birds snatch winter berries from the wind,
wires sing, their slow hymns drifting
over blown-flat fields of snow.

The man brings nothing except a face
stripped bare, hands empty of
everything but laughter's snare.

Trees shake off the yellow brevities
of spring, tremble in the first dearth
of winter's siege and suck at earth.

The man welcomes you to your own home,
to this country you thought was yours;
you note his soft, familiar way with words.

Sky blanches to a precipice your blood
can't climb or pass; snow lies against
window ledges, whispers on glass.

The man cancels refusals from your face;
he conjures papers and conceals a gun;
he offers you terms on this house you own.

At once you see a dream of this:
lines of pilgrims in trudging streams,
lice following a warm shirt's seams.

The man switches all the house lights on,
he sighs into a fireside chair, he draws
you close and strokes your hair.

Outside a wren jerks its agate eyes,
jabbing at the rowan fruit's red rind
where washing stiffens in the wind.

Soon you'll walk from the house and turn
from the land, you'll run from every stick
and stone and every neighbour's hand.

The man shakes his head, regretting the
trust he placed in you, not laughing now, but
needling a number on your arm in faintest blue.

SOUTHBOUND

Last night we went missing from
the world, had to drag sleep's
drowning to surface for this train,
southbound, late and slow as a cortège.

Pigeons flocked into apricot clouds
from the station's roof of glass;
we walked the platform, rolled newspapers
into wads and thumped our legs.

Now there's rain, the train swishing
over sleepers, the conductor reciting
his poem of destinations, warming each
town's cold consonants Jamaican-style.

At Warrington chimneys spindle
the mist, spinning hanks of smoke;
the track's drawn threads gleam under
a gnawed moon's waning into day.

Those travellers watch us and wait,
their breath white, their faces
vague as ingots cooling in a tank.
We judder on the squeal of brakes

slip into the suction of gathering light.
A woman eats her yoghurt with a silver key,
a man spins a yellow pear,
that girl sleeps with folded hands

and will wake soon to make her face.
Rain flecks the windows, slakes
dried sorrel in fields below where
a white mare runs by the fence

flicking back her head
from the brink of our din.
A signalman stares from his lit box,
hands parting the track, neat

as sugar tongs to send us south.
The conductor's voice comes again, its hymn
sing-song and sorrowful, pronouncing each
place's name until we're almost sure it's there.

DANDELIONS

They'll grow anywhere, dandelions,
their seeds flocking to a mist,
swarming in faint dreams of light
from a far dimension of Space,
weaving the sheer silk of air,
staining it to watered milk.

They settle on our shoulders,
on the roofs of cars or houses,
on gravel paths, or by the roadside;
you wouldn't rate their chances higher
than icicles in hell.

But in spring they come through:
obvious things forgotten, which suddenly
are remembering themselves everywhere,
rising through damp soil and cold and rain,
through fretted autumn leaves,
the lengthening days' light.

They take over garden paths,
flower beds, verges, window boxes;
they punch through tarmac in the street,
their tap roots spiking into graveyards
to rock the headstones, their faces
brightening the names of the dead.

The first flowers I took my mother
were dandelions,
snapping a fistful of stems,
their sap trickling down my wrist,
sticky as sperm,
their yellow heads oozing a faint
scent of piss and bitterness.

I smelled the space between their lives
and mine.

This one clings to the outhouse roof,
gulping in heat from the May sun
with grateful little nods,
downy as a new duckling,
it's baby head lolling
in a faint breeze
that teases it to fall.

Tomorrow's wind will strip you,
tear out that gloss of fibres,
your bald pod drying to a husk,
your root slumbering between slates,
under winter stars - their suddenly
blooming flowers of frost.

In spring you'll pull the house down,
or try to.

If I'm here, and you make it,
I'll come down one day, woken by
the hunger of starlings, taking in
today's milk from the doorstep,
yesterday's news from the paper,
to find you, suddenly overripe.

THE ICE CREAM MAN

Here comes the evening ice-cream man,
turning the hurdy-gurdy higher,
nudging the kerb with the ice-cream van:
we hear the squeal of its fat black tyre.

Is it that his eyes are too yellow,
the hair on his arms too coarse and rough
to play the part of the ice-cream seller?
When he speaks his voice is low and gruff.

But he greets the children with a kind '*hello*',
scooping their wishes from the frozen tub;
he warns them of traffic and watches them go,
his lips sucking smoke from a cigarette stub.

The children who queue there do not know
that his mind is a darkened cinema
where old Pathé newsreels flicker and glow:
the salute, the eagle, the swastika.

He has a whole shelf of books on the Reich,
a patent black leather belt and boots,
a model machine-gun, a motor-bike,
and a wife whose hair is blonde to the roots.

He watches the Führer speak each night,
the uniforms massed in the heaving stands;
when applause explodes the pigeons to flight
they wheel like a flock of clapping hands.

And he's even clapped his own hands numb
at meetings held in those secret places
where real-life fascists from Germany come
to help cleanse the country of non-white faces.

Under the counter where he puts the coins
are photographs taken through Belsen's wire:
the skeletal ribs, the wasted loins
excite him with itchy sweats of desire

that make his shaking hands clench tight.
The needle of hate is climbing the dial
and we see, as the dusk turns into night,
what he means by that feral ghost of a smile.

The street is empty, the blinds are rolled,
but he plays the music for one more taker,
his fingers are bruised purple with cold –
like the butcher, the baker, the candle-stick maker.

INHERITANCE

He watched the first snowflakes abseil
into the yard's stink, melting on dung
he'd forked there, making the farm dogs
whimper, yelp, snatch at their chains.

That morning lapwings had dropped into the fields,
surprising him with their jester's flight:
too early for spring, the wind was in the north
and each bud a blackened tip of steel.

The week before he'd watched cherry blossom
in the graveyard. Now this wind would strip each
branch to its filament, its wake of frost
clamp shut the throats of crocuses.

Last night the sun had fallen slobbering
at the red lips of clouds, pleading
to be out into the bloody world;
it sank unheeded and with it sank the light.

Then the wind had moved a compass point,
its anticyclone whorling over the North Sea,
bringing its inheritance of cold to dull him –
like uncashable war-bonds, the Fordson, the land.

It frayed his knuckles where he worked the fields'
need of him, walling up gaps where frost
and thaw had shunted stone downhill
to let his pregnant ewes stumble through.

It froze the promise in his mouth, stung
him with hailstones' unrelenting kisses.
She was in the valley, bellyful of his child,
a thin acre of this farm already sown in her.

That night, alone, he cradled his head
at the fire, smelling sweet muck dry in its heat;
alone, letting the wind go over the fell,
the river glitter towards imagined cities.

He went outside to lean against a solid wall
of cold, blinking the Plough's stars from his eyes,
letting the door creak on its hinge of light,
his breath drift, white as a moth's flight.

TRAVELOGUE IN CIRCULAR BREATHING

Dolan driving to another job balances the map
on the steering wheel, changes down for the ring-road,
for another sales-pitch steepening with every year of soft-
soaping a living from discount stores, bars and corner shops.

He parks on the gravel forecourt: another hotel with
oil-sump breakfasts and plastic en-suite bathroom doors,
no vacancies, but tv's left on all night by legless
middle-managers asleep in crumpled suits as snow
falls on the town and the river blackens the weir.

Dolan drops his bag, pisses, yawns into the mirror, stares
through curtains to check his watch against the only local
legend here: four church clocks keeping four wrong times.

Dolan brews up an instant tea, adds whitener, thinks
of cows drooling to milking parlours through the frost
of churned fields, their burning breath figuring a woman
in jodhpurs he used to fuck on a farm when he was younger
in a bigger car, her old man harvesting peas as they sweated
in bed, working at a climax like he'd work at sales figures
or persuasive charm.

That last time she'd slammed the door, white-faced,
whispering *go away*, away because her life had crashed
back into place where it belonged under the neighbours'
gossip and glaucous, potato-picking eyes; he knew why
that came but never how.

Dolan lies down, relishing breast-weight and buttock-
curve, her neck and perfume, her wet mouth on his
and cries for more in summer heat that sent them crazy,
upturning furniture and bedroom rugs. Dolan trying to
remember hugs the pillow where the smell of someone
else's cigarettes not quite laundered from the sheets
tugs him to the present moment on its leash.

He needs a drink. No problem – anything he wants here
where he's known by name, another balding rep in striped
shirts and cheap shoes, his car lined up outside with the others
like wives over-dressed for functions where the men are given
golf-clubs, gold-watches or holidays in Spain for simply being
where they had to be and doing what was done.

Dolan in the bar feeling smaller and older than he should
is secretly twice the man these younger bastards ever were,
boasting of iron-pumping, blowjobs and fuel injection in
voices sadder than that fifty year-old child's in the hostel across
the street, yodelling at the night like a dingo or didgeridoo –
on and on, Jesus, on and on – which reminds Dolan
of circular breathing, that someone once told him the way
the trick was done; exactly how he's forgotten now, but
still feels pride in something once known.

Traffic goes past in the rain, the sound of someone sweeping
a floor or sanding a box; headlights slide across the ceiling
of room seven, searching for something or someone lost.
Dolan shifting to switch on the news spills tea down his shirt,
dabs it with the bedspread that smells of smoke, hearing
the man-child's broken voice howl down a fat moon from
cloud-gaps over the hostel garden.

Later in the Chinese takeaway Dolan watches goldfish
circling a tank wondering if the woman he saw yesterday
shaking rain from her hair at a bus-stop is still there some-
where as the fish spiral finning the glass and sucking up
the gravel with oriental calm until he's tired of their slow
exotic ease of hearing the girl with black hair and eyes no
older than his own daughter and too polite to shout asking
him over and over round and round what he wants *please*.

MACHAIR

Sky is widest here, the sea
coldest against that dream of sand,
its white cuticle curving away.

A sycamore turns pale,
it sways like a tall woman
helplessly dancing.

A buoy rots in the marram,
luring that wrecked hull,
that tractor buried in pebbles

to its surf of rust.
Meadows of clover and buttercup
crumble at the beach where dunlin

feed, frenetic as roaches.
The tide hauls ropes of weed,
plovers call out with larks

and meadow pipits –
a multitude that could be heavenly
but the looted crofts, the undug

lazybeds say otherwise.
Uist men drive cattle in Paraguay,
steer cargoes out from Cape Breton,

the Gaelic snagging their tongues
with names and custom, tattered
as feedbags on barbed wire.

The waves drag at beer-cans,
sea-boots, a torn fishing net,
boiler-plates tumble in the backwash

and a Bedford van slips on the cliff.
Last night a seal came like a lost
dog to watch the land for humans

and found us, trudging at the *machair*,
trying to match oyster catchers' cries
with wrong words, the wrong language.

VALENTINE

Today I burn a mouse for you,
burn it because you rose early
and found it already dead
on the bathroom floor –
unexpected and frightening you said –
dozing again, that way you have of
talking in your sleep and waking me.

A small task; I give this mouse
to the shrivel of flame and smoke,
no stigmata on its hands, no sweat
of forgiveness or ironic vines across
its holy brow, but this mouth-shaped
wound in its side cannot be ignored
and bleeds like hidden kingliness.

Today I burn a mouse for you, burn it
like a late-fallen leaf, wondering
at the moment of its death, tripping
over spring's doorstep into sudden winter;
let our hearth mourn this the only way
it can - with heat, purifying fire,
with sulphur in its saffron temple.

A mouse dies unexpectedly, frightening
all the clocks in the house, which mutter
like footsteps over pontoon bridges,
out of step in case the whole thing fails;
take it, you said, *take it,*
these words somehow more distinct
than anything, so much clearer
than prayers I can't remember or recite.

Today I burn a mouse for you, burn
it in the stillness of this house
where the pipes murmur and light rises
at the windows, where you still dream

its sly scamper and rodent mirth,
its paws in the butter dish or
scooping up a manna of spilled oats
or weaving a nest in the sofa-back.

Today I burn a mouse for you
and only smoke slips between us
like the vaguest word for love.

THE HURTS

To Lethe On the 8-10

A weak dawn drowns all England under mist,
this train rocks us in its glass cradle
against the track where steel wheels hiss,
a slick of water glimmers on the pylons' cable.
Trees stand out as skeins of blackened wire,
the windows show us staring at our faces,
mist spreads, choking out the sun's ash-fire,
the stations' names christen nameless places.
That young couple are joined hand in hand,
he sleeps against her and she strokes his head,
he wakes to see pale fogs inhale the land,
white grasses that the winter leaves for dead.
The girder bridge flits by like a lantern show,
the river drinks our lights in darkness far below.

Octoberscape

Last night was breathless here, trees
dropped their leaves in dusky stillness
sheer as the underslip silking your knees
or the inheld gasp of my caress.
Today the path is a dross of sycamore's
yellow stars, the woodland burns
with beeches, a soot of crows floats
above their flames and slowly turns.
The air is indrawn, so still a film of dust
scums the lake where coot and mallard dive,
trees rustle naked, their sound so soft
it intimates our whispered cries of love.
Last night you wept and threw your shoe against my face;
today I search for where we lay but cannot find the place.

Red Shin Cove

Holy Island glimmers faintly to the south,
its silver mirage trembles under wind
that raises sand to sting our mouths
and bury footprints that we leave behind.
Two girls play, half-naked in the sea,
cormorants fly low, terns dive then
wavecrests fling them to my searching eye –
this beach is ground from creatures once alive.
A tanker passes slowly, heading east to
where the sky has dunked itself in blues,
the waves ferment against our feet, their yeast
of salt will dry and whiten on our shoes.
At dusk I'll light a fire of driftwood in the sand,
pour broken shells and promises into your hand.

Axe

The axe speaks clearly to the wood,
its steel tongue thuds along the grain,
the halves drop cleanly if the line is good
and if the head is truly aimed.
This log has knots where offshoots grew,
the axe falls, stammers, then sticks.
My wrist is numbed through – blood to bone –
though it should be wise to timber's tricks.
You're watching from the window with our child,
your lips leafing a brief, subtle smile;
each dumb blow entangles me, until I've used
up every angle, all my guile.
The verbs and nouns of steel will never part
a wood so knotted, inarticulate.

Burn Moor

Night has scorched the heather roots ash white
and every rock is pale with crystal dust,
cold has hulled the tarns, all night
fixing plates of ice, rivets of frost.
The purple hills are vague, seem to burn
beyond this mist that we are stumbling in;
adders are asleep beneath these stones,
veiled in the venom-diamonds of their skin.
The quaking bog's a frozen crust of grass
where grouse's wings explode their panic-blur,
wind goads us speechless with its lash,
sky sloughs the sun – a moon's faint replica.
Frost crystals blow and hiss upon the stones,
we turn for home and find our footprints gone.

Alone

You're three days gone away – at first the space
you left was small and I was free inside it.
Now that you're coming back, your hands, your face,
your eyes invade my sleep and wake me
to this absence. Cold has whitened all the roofs,
which the sun licks damp and black, a fire-cat
lapping up the sleeping town where proof that we
exist at all is scarce as letters on the mat.
No letters come, no sad voice shimmers
down a cackling line – too far away, too lost
for that. I dust your shoes, polish off last glimmers
of the window's funeral-parlour leaves of frost.
The hours between us are dull sleepers: they let pass
steel lines, your train, you dozing in its chrysalis.

Words

Words wait, just as minerals sleep in stone
to be washed out slowly by the rain;
their crystals interlock and they alone
can articulate the facets of our pain.
They glint in sun's temporary light,
the brief visitation that lets bloom
Earth's breathing green, our own delight
in words that even humanise a sterile moon.
Each brilliant syllable in space
will turn and fall dumb to the light;
every kiss I'll ever burn into your face
will cool and fade. You'll forget tonight
but it doesn't matter, we'll die anyhow:
it matters that we feel the hurt of loving now.

A NIGHT ON THE LASH

MY FATHER'S FIRST DAY AT WORK

Half asleep in the grey smudge of September
rain a carthorse sneezes towards fleeting
dazzles of the sun.

Its hooves click on a cobbled yard, its hide
flinches from my hand and rain trails its silver
filaments from tilted hooves.

The horse dreams me from its sweat of sleep
or I dream the horse, the day itself,
that smell of soap and leather,

a fly entering its nostril, this mane tangling
my fingers, the way its neck is coarse, hot,
and kissable with rain.

If I try to look away from these lost days
a boy distracts me, enters the yard
to set down pails of milk

and smiles towards me through a looming war
and does not recognise me and hardly tastes
the bit of work between his teeth.

ECLIPSE

You're back tonight. Outside my door,
your face dark through its frost.

It's thirst that brings you; don't pretend
otherwise. Your lips are dry.

Tonight only the moon is quenchable.
We watch from the window's slit:

its fist salutes from the mountain's
epaulets of snow.

The moon bounds, the street brightens
under lost gravity.

Moon is pure meniscus, water's gleam
in a well's sleeve.

The night digs its own long shadow,
spades it into that hole.

Our duel is on again, you say. The moon's
tossed dollar turns on its

shot-out rim. Your mouth is hot. Now
blood marbles the moon

its mist spreading in fine droplets
sprayed from our kiss.

Stars' shrapnel cools, still white-hot,
still screaming outwards.

Before you slept I saw the orange
moon clear like lipstick

smeared from a mirror. Before you woke
a whole night later, I saw

a shadow tremble on your eye then fall,
splashing into moon.

DISTANCE

Gridlocked, the station broils in lassitude;
rails glint in angle-grinding sun, girls saunter
in short skirts, a porter shunts trolleys, a cat
woos pigeons with disingenuous charm.

No train. The town is held at two o'clock, no ransom
for its golden hands, but girls still pass, so something
must be happening somewhere close. The cat cocks
its ears and stares, the porter wipes his face, the woman

sighs, the man rubs stubble, fumbles for a match.
Headlines wilt on the news stand, calamities
settle into columns, calmed until we read them,
feel something – nothing maybe – treading

two o'clock like water deeper than our legs.
You're screwing your heel into pink chewing
gum, sighing in your yellow frock. Elsewhere,
the train shimmers in its chemise of heat,

I smoke this cigarette, watch your breasts pant
under their glaze of salt. I'm through with kissing you,
I think, but can't say exactly why or what has snapped
loose from its attenuated moment. Pigeons parachute

from gutters, the town hall time is two, the train arrives.
I watch those girls watch a woman ask a man a question
which slakes his face the way dust takes rain. Your eyes
brim with slamming doors and you're asking me again,

What's wrong? What's wrong?
All this, I say, taking your arm, taking the pulse
of your body's closeness to mine, its distance
from the sun. *All this*.

WALKING HOME ON NEW YEAR'S DAY

Two am. First-footing a whitened road,
hills gleaming with ice, hoar frost
curdled on each wall and iron gate.

Earth skates under Orion's belt,
the road sways, the moon sinks,
licked away by ebbing dark.

Sheep cough in fields of tarnished light,
snow just holding back its mass
of purest sleep, the uncertain edge

of wakefulness we're walking now.
I tell you something strange and wonderful
to pass the time: how water frozen

under zero's brink can still stay fluid
against all odds, how its molecules
cheat Nature's laws, brimming

at the very frontier of solidity, like old
men slugging strokes against the
deepening current of their lives.

Supercool superfluity of motion: a miracle!
Until one snowflake falls to slush whole
lakes into the stillest blues of instant ice.

It's said our Universe could hold its own
dark matter in such breath-held states, that
any particle colliding there could in a blink

unpick the cross-stitch of the stars.
We pause to think about those aeons of ice,
mull a slow kiss spiced with wine –

annunciation that we'll never change or die.
I pull away, walk on, look up to feel the first
snowflake landing on my eye.

BLACK DOG

The dog is watching your house, the black dog in
the grass of sorrows, down on four paws, staring
as thunderheads gather, watching for a gleam
of lights, some wild expectancy of curtains pulled

or song snatched or steps waltzed above dawn's
apricot abyss. The black dog points its ears,
snuffles a wind of scent-whorls, hears the radio, a
turning page, your heart in quiet rooms, a knife

against bread, a spoon clinking an empty cup; it
smells your sweat, hand-printed on the mail, and
something else, close to fear or nakedness. A new
day fills rooms with dread of mawkish tunes or her

hand slanted on an envelope. The dog lies doggo,
Mnemosyne clamped in its mouth, that willing bitch.
The turned page is blank; music drops like a vase,
ivy blows against the window, its inane metre

counting to nothing, night and day. The dog runs from
a dream of welted black, lopes through inky streams,
leaps a creosoted fence, an oil-skimmed ditch, gallops a
marsh of burning tar. Brought by a call above hearing's

pitch, the dog keeps vigil and when admitted to the
house, stinks of rain, wet hair, sour yeast and shit.
This sable hound shakes silver from its coat; you
feed it from a crazed blue bowl, stroke its narrow skull

where you exist in analogues of sound and scent.
The dog is dark as a full-stop or a clot of feeding flies;
it could be shot or gassed or pricked to sleep. That
thought's no use. The dog's eyes fill with amber light

that tents you on twin globes. You're in too deep,
door-stepped by the tenth and most reliable muse.

DEMAGNETISED

You fumble a takeaway foil tray
onto the oil-dark chaos of his desk;
one Madras chicken, a garlic naan
his revved-up pancreas might risk.

His morning's spent on a mobile phone
copper-greasing metal deals; outside
the lads strip out each wreck from
glove compartments to the wheels.

The cabin's piled with wiper-blades,
acid-free batteries, radio-cassettes
that spew tape like you'll spill your guts
about this bastard's bag of tricks.

A Gilletted ear leaks rubies as he drops
his bucket mouth and bolts the lot,
then spanners out one rusty benediction:
This fucking bastard's fucking hot.

The crane glissands an Escort past –
God, pity his wife is all you think –
its crumpled bonnet's dumped, crushed,
then cubed into a neatened life.

The boss hoists his balls, belches,
scraps his tinsel plate and farts;
windscreen crystal snows like tears
freezing over broken hearts.

Later, you'll scrawl his name on his
unfunny, photocopied arse, pin it to
the bulletin board he rates so smart,
then update his logbook, getting in

each time and place he never rendered
unto the Revenue what was due;
anonymous, you stitch him up for each
time he had then disregarded you.

Sun's low-beam lights up camomile,
its petals drooping, Arctic White;
that Nova's willing mascot nods,
then crashes as the magnetism's cut.

Off to the post, you watch the lads renew
a resprayed ringer's everlasting life;
winching in an engine, welding seats,
erasing chassis numbers with a knife.

The clock glides back over motorways,
near-misses, still days, country lanes
and lay-by lovemaking it never registered:
that row of noughts makes everything begin again.

MYSON MIDAS

At first it worked like a clock, the timer's plastic
teeth gritted in the day's hours to vent that puff of
steam each dawn: a gun to raise the drowned.

Then radiators ticking, water climbing the house,
a wash of heat that dried the air, warped window-
frames and kept us from the snow. One day it

stalled, monarchical and crazed, boiling paint-blisters
until the gas-man calmed it, his hands soothing it
the way a shepherd lambs a softly bleating ewe.

It sulked for weeks. The gas-man almost lodged with
us: checked resistances, changed sensors, untangled
wiring looms, fingered pipes to track a fading pulse.

Intermittent faults are hard to find. Too true. What he
couldn't guess, his hands groped for in gloom lit by
rubies on the diode board. He felt a drip and

staunched it, clipped strands of copper, coaxed
gaskets, Morsed free a sticking valve, and with a fine-
haired brush did archaeology on seams of dust.

Dog-days of random heat ensued; we never knew what
happened when we left the house, if scalding plumes or
flutters of the pilot flame erupted there to flare and cool.

One day I found him, head-pressed to the boiler's guts,
swearing in iambics *at the bastard thing*, his hands em-
bedded, coaxing hope. They came out carbon-stained

but cupped success: a ghost-flame lit his worn, angelic face.
He left for good; an absence; idling heat. Now, at two-am
a taxi tracks the street. Someone steps home alone to

bear their empty house. We lie awake, touch fingertips, hear rooms exhale last whispers of the miracle his hands have brailled here for our fumbling hands to read.

MOTH AT LLANÇÁ

All night circling, its antennae feathering
against blinds, wings ticking on white walls
where we lie in memories of our lives.

Then grasshoppers staving our pillows with
insomniac haste, as if we lay until dawn
in a sea's long fever of unrest.

The bread van mutters smoke, sounds its horn;
our shoulders touch, burned by a fallen sun.
Sheets lie in a heap, their cotton rumpled

like the mountain outside, still asleep.
Air sings. The moth on the sill, face-down,
folds death's head in its wings.

GENERAL PINOCHET, RETIRED

He tidies the lawn, scuffs toadstools with
his heel, rakes them like a mare's flank,
then wanders from the sun.

Nights have gnawed the apple to a gourd;
it brings ants which scatter on the table
until his finger stops their run for it.

The same finger strops dew from a crow's
feather, which he arranges with the apple
into the stillest life.

He reads a newspaper, strokes the table's
planed narrative of seasons, regards
the pale shades of his infamy.

He listens to the maid in the kitchen, lets
his finger drift to the feather, pictures
wing-tips spiralling into light.

He's thirsty from his work, calls her to
bring him lemon juice, iced water beading
a glass. But she is busy some-

where behind him, salting almonds,
slicing limes, singing to no one
of Iquique's bone-dry winds.

FERAL

Footloose, it gathers impressions faithlessly,
defining things which remain undefined, not
seeking love nor expecting it, but expert
in similitude.

Describing breakers on a beach then riding them,
a tideline of frayed plastic, gulls' cries, then dusk
in which a human voice is broken
to the point of tears.

The next moment seducing out the scents of thyme
or tar or rotting fish, the touch of wet ferns or fresh-
tasting figs and every part of speech
brindling with appetite.

Slinking through sleeping towns, licking its paws,
napping in the undertaker's doorway, waking
for star-rise, stretching, noting the anguish
in a hurrying woman's heels.

Then the tricks of darkness across rooftops where
shadows lurch and breed; the assignation
of each thing with words and its turning
back to dumbness.

On the move again over damp lawns, under
hung sheets sagged by dew or frost, watching
a fox redden the golf course, rooks gathering
for early mass, a girl's stark body rolled

from a car into the future's chilled forensics.
Then padding across a bridge too frail to
take its weight, alert in each sense, intent
on everything and fiercely satisfied.

Leaping from roof to roof, moving over streets
and under them, escaping notice, arching its
back at its own scream shocked onto
a pane of blackened glass.

Would you trust it, take such a creature home?
To purr the days away, lie flat as the pages
in a book? Then out all night and fucking
so wild it sounds like death?

Lapping the moon from a saucer, licking its neck-fur,
hypocrisy's winding-gear grinding in its throat,
soliciting your hand, your love, your kitchen's
offal, heat, and blood.

Now ignoring you: hesitant, decisive, fey, its pupils
slashed in irises green as jealousy or jade,
its footsteps hardly rhyming
as it pads away.

A HOLE FOR BELGRADE

First a dimple, then a crater, then tarmac cancer gnawing
its way from light like something the council or God
laid on without the usual paperwork.

Then a man with halitosis and a measuring wheel,
the sound of running water that might always
have been there. You can never tell.

That surprises him more than missiles hitting Belgrade,
mass graves turned over, an iron plough in his hands
as he dreams the news each night.

This year he shrugs off May blossom, ignores rhubarb,
beheads daffodils with scarcely a word to his neighbour –
the baker with a Polish past.

No one takes the hole away, which after all is only half
a hole; and who knows when a hole has stopped
growing, or just when half a life has passed?

Lying beside his wife at night who smells of hair dye, hot
nylon, unreachable loneliness, he sees the hole
as a suddenly emptied mouth.

Almighty Father. He skims in beautiful words, remembered
prayers, one childhood song in which *The big ship sails
through the ally, ally-o, the*

hole caves in, surprising him again - its lack of warning.
How can it do that? he asks his wife,
First nothing, then a hole?

She's wiping marmalade from her moustache, thinking
how she'd sliced oranges in a hot kitchen last
autumn, seduced the baker she hadn't known

was Catholic, until he came gasping Hail Mary's full
of grace. That night her husband lies puzzling over
the thought of taking lives to save them.

Then the sound of lorries, the council digger, hard-core
being tipped, arc lights, voices and a spade
scraping at his nerves.

But council men at night? *At night?* They leave the hole half-
filled, a plastic fence in place, chalk marks on the road -
the kind that spare the first-born.

Five daily papers later, nothing's changed, except more
rubble in Belgrade, more pictures of the dead unburying
themselves with newsprint blackened hands.

He watches the hole, there in the road, unhealed.
You'll stay, he says, *For ever and ever. You'll stay.*
Amen.

AMNIOCENTESIS

Kerry hills' piled turves smouldering;
far off rain, thunderclouds, a mackerel
spine of light splitting over sand.

Packing a few things, flinching
from a bumble bee, sun on her
arms, the road a necessary
scar on the day.

Sea's pewter tongues licking
away the strand; then a skylark
falling silent, then a knife chopping
sage in the kitchen where her sister
is helping out.

Cut lemons, zest, haste;
the sea's swell a vast
optimistic lie, the windows
repeating her every move.

Her shoulder scalding with
impossible sun, the mountains
put there to tell her:
Live with this.

Fuchsia, montbretia, willowherb;
the sea murmuring, stammering
to pronounce itself at the edge
of things –
soon, now, the road
soon, now, the road –
this memory still happening,
and will not stop.

WASHDAYS

A washtub, a washboard, a hot yard,
the man's anger chipping at bricks,
drawing his bride through her mangle
in the washday sun.

A lead pipe spurting at a grid where
slugs copulate in grease; the mill
chimney writing something high up
in smoke they can't yet read.

The man searching for work, the
wound under his demob suit itching,
its metal splinters burrowing towards
his lung. Then words blurting, then

the man's hand across the woman's
face, unexpected, like her tears;
everything here unexpected, except
poverty the end of war prophesied.

Womb-blood on a towel, the woman
washing it away with green soap eked
from ration coupons; only blood and
her husband's voice unrationed now.

A window gawping from the house,
the man's mother staring out, gauging
whiteness, an insufficiency of sweat
sudding the washboard. Each Tuesday,

the woman dabbing Dolly Blue on the man's
collars; then a child in her belly, sloshing as
she sways to the wash, away from the man's
voice, his speech fracturing, incomplete –

like the night never quite closing over her,
sleepless on pillows stuffed with down,
her head on a flock of birds snatched
from their fidelities in a far-off sea of ice.

The man hoisting the wet basket,
too heavy for her condition, their
sheets bleaching them out from the day,
their voices disappearing into sun,

vanishing from the room where his
mother hoards shillings in an Oxo tin,
spiders at another inquisition about her belly,
shopping bills, the Co-op divvy.

The wife stoops, takes a clutch of lupins
to his mother's sneered surety she'll
fill the house with bad luck or bastards;
instead she brings colours, warping light.

The old woman sulks by the wireless,
dwelling on free teeth, a pension, her own
husband sucked down into Ypres mud,
still young in his unmarked grave.

The woman remembers her own dead
mother dusting at a worn settee,
worshipping the front step, a donkey
stone yellowing decencies underfoot.

The man talks, his voice harping on lino,
distemper, a stairs-runner; the woman
arranging lupins in a scraped out jar,
the man's voice a rolling boil, his fingers

daily shaming her face. The woman,
imagines the child, not crying for it yet
because there is everything to cry for,
because tears are commonplace, like

ashes cast out each morning to the
dirt back where the child will play.
Once she helped a soldier die, his last
words nothing she could understand;

just another nurse, but her own soldier
lived, watched her from his bed as they
gathered around him, cooling his wound-
fever with starched white wings.

Now that wound twists his mouth, stitching
it with crooked speech. He never tried
to kill, he says, pointing the rifle anywhere,
letting it kick above his heart where

only hymns had kicked before. Then he
lay in rubble, hit; no pain, but fire blackening
him the way a belt buckle tarnishes,
the way a wound grows gangrenous.

She'd seen that too: a homesick, southern
GI boy smiling through a stench they couldn't
bear until he slipped away through choked
French verbs to the bayou's cloying dark.

These memories: the woman sitting with her face
in lupins; the man idling; the mother of the man
afraid in her own changed house; their washing
towing the garden into brightening wind.

Sun is machined into its lathe-cut arc;
the window cooling the woman's temple,
sky ravelling out an unspun hank of smoke
to swaddle the hootered town.

Days, seasons, nights. The earth dizzy,
the moon untrodden, acid from factory
chimneys rotting bricks and slate, the town
dying and growing, bringing the city's

overspill to new estates where they'll covet
a council semi, freeze his mother with a box
Brownie then bury her in the Baptist church,
her mouth pursed tight as cash.

It goes on: days wrapping them in rain, in
sun, in breath. The boy-child at ease under
her heart, his blood kicking at the cord, his
clenched fists already sure of everything.

THE ALCHEMIST NEXT DOOR

What he does, you wonder, hearing
him clatter quietly to his wheelie bin
on dark mornings, fumbling with black bags
when the sky is pure frozen sleep.

All night his house lights burn and you
picture him at a table etching crystals
from dull stone, their brilliance ringing
his eyes with amethyst.

Or when the bags squelch see him
butchering body parts, hands bloody,
his bedroom an abattoir, his fridge a
skull-house, backlit and grinning.

On cold days his starter-motor rasps
abraded splines, starts at the third try
when he drives off to some kind of work,
wiping the windscreen with a rag.

Or never works, but parks to watch
the windows of a certain house where
a woman drowns her face in silvered glass
and hums the cadence in his head.

You couldn't draw his face from memory
yet at weekends greet him, amiably
scooping the sundae of a frozen rose bed,
astonished by the paleness of his hands.

He watches you watching him alone,
the way your eyes absent themselves,
searching his soil for sharp serifs,
its sanskrit of fallen petals or of bone.

A NIGHT ON THE LASH

The river's neon blusher is rising through rain,
through sewers and gutters and cast-iron grids,

through faked alibis, failed marriages, through
suicide and homicide and fumbled, sad affairs.

She's out alone tonight, lounging on a high stool,
wanting something more than this,

eye-lashes lowered, cheekbones cool against
a chromium rail. A single rum, her fingers

slack on the glass, her stacked heels rising
and falling with that song. Those lads

laughing in the back room, spinning pool
queues, strutting to the jukebox, born to

the manner, the lash, to everlasting pints
of Stella, baseball caps, unlaced trainers,

jeans loose against designer groins.
The lash cracks rain on glass, the river

glitters up slimed brickwork, plucking at
each streetlight's yellow blossom.

Blatant lips, an emptied glass, ice melting
the bar stool's itch against her thighs; her short

dress, parted breasts, the lads laughing at nothing,
but something pressing with its insistence to be

somewhere and someone. The lash coiling, her
tongue dipping, the last drop, the jukebox

telling us to dance or die, her fingernails
smoothing hair under the lights' hot knife.

Then the lads standing in a line, still laughing,
lashing the porcelain, asking dumbly

Is this what it means, to dance or die?
If only they could speak, lad to lad, but can't,

returning for another round to find that lass,
that slapper gagging for it, gone.

Gone into rain, into the mythology of Friday night
sex that never happened yet like this.

They lash down a pint, then another; she traces
sweat down a taxi window. *Where to, love?*

wakes her, the driver smiling at his meter,
slackening his turban where she'd like

to lay the lash of fuscia lips, loosen his rope
of oiled hair, then lower herself to meet

the river's rise. But listen: she's whispering,
she's whispering. *To anywhere.*

PRODIGAL

The house anticipates you, its memory
bringing it from blown mist at the lane-end
where litter is caught on a hedge
and your father's car rages into rust.

Approach by apple trees where spiders
have webbed branches with a morning's
fine brocade of pearls; they part for you,
an avenue of veiled, expectant brides.

First sparrows hunger under dawn's
uncrumpled sheets of silk; no stirrings
from the house, though one light left on
still signals from a room of books.

An hour's wait. Quotidian things amaze:
the radio's blurred tongue, the scent of
burning toast, the swish of curtain rings,
your father's voice the same.

Your mother rises to her children's milk-
teeth smiles, shrugs into a damson
dressing gown – that Christmas gift – clearing
her hair from its collar, careless as a girl.

Here is the house: its spare-room duvet
folded back, its cupboard of broken toys,
bicycles outgrown in the garden shed, a
half-built glider hanging in the attic room.

Lives resume, grow back towards themselves
the way house-plants grope for light; now
rays delineate the lawn, dowse a gutter, gild
the door knocker where your hand tries

to rap an entrance but falls away instead.
This house with its coffee cups, its blue fume
of iris in a vase, its hush of order. The way they
rush to the phone, catching a child's voice

in the man's, anxious for everything in lives
that rushed past theirs. Go in. This is your
room, rearranging its furniture over plain rugs,
hanging old pictures on new-painted walls.

Go in to take your mother's tears, your father's
paper hand, their questions abbreviating a
journey of lost years to this moment in a place
you need to stay but can't, and cannot need.

Sweat awake at night, grope for a glass
where the fridge hums incantations of ice,
where thoughts melt to a water-stain map
of somewhere else you'd like to be.

In the morning, mist clamps the trees again,
your mother steams creases from a blouse,
your father whistles from the garden, tending
a fire of leaves which hardly yet begin to fall.

This house where nothing happens now,
freighted with forgiveness. This house of
open doors, and broken bread. This house
where you must wake and learn to breathe again.

THORPENESSE

Here at the world's edge the moon was almost full
last night, dragging its trail across the sea, pulling
stunned water into shingle's finned arêtes.

It laid a tide of flotsam at the beach: bladderwrack,
dismembered crabs, cuttlefish, driftwood, turds of
engine oil, peat-cobs, a woman's shoe cargoed by

longshore drift. Now a message in a bottle weighted
with stones. It must have bobbed gleaming in that
glare of moon as we made love so unexpectedly,

fallen into sleep until the edges of our dreams touched
to wake us. Afterwards, we rose, opened curtains,
watched a trawler lit from bow to stern riding out the

swell, its fairground gaiety stilled by salt, night's depth,
uncertain dark. The treasure map parts in your hands,
shows a skull, crossed bones, a windmill, the marsh

where whatever is buried sinks under its portentous
scarlet cross. The way things look it didn't get far, just
lilted back to the same beach; maybe those kids knew

the sleight-of-hand of tides and planned it this way,
or maybe hoped to beach their riddle someplace far off
they imagined a curious people were, eyes turned to

the cult of equinoctial seas. Curious, the way last night
I laid my ear to your breastbone to find what I've always
sought beyond fathomable skin, your deft hands

signalling unsaid things. I heard blood ebbing then rising
with each emission of your heart, that's all. Today we're
gathering sea-coal, spars of jet, amber and amethyst.

Waves furl, rub pebbles into grains of scarcely diminished
time, infinite worlds whose horizons can't hide the ancient
stare of newness in the dawn. The sea glitters, a fishing boat

drops its nets. You're signalling another find, waving from
the spray of a clouded sky towards something far out
for which words have blown over or away.

NOTES ON THE LONDON UNDERGROUND

We float face-up in windows on the Tube,
past cables pumped-out like a junkie's arm;
no talk, just wheels on steel, the hiss of
brakes pressing with their insane calm.

Workmen in Day-Glo orange coats are here,
restoring something among ghostly crowds;
above this tunnel's held-back tons of clay
are city spires still reaching for the clouds.

Madonna of wraiths, that woman paints her lips,
a mirror pixillates to dust-motes in her palm –
event-horizon of a hole we travel in, not through.
She dabs on mascara's voodoo charm.

Brake linings burn, we stall, shunt forward,
touch, avoid each other's eyes or stare where
hoardings sell the city to itself, until Bacardi,
Coke, and Palm Beach holidays become a blur.

At Charing Cross we step through shushing
doors into a prickly, feral heat. There's nowhere
now to go but up; we file through turnstiles,
spill as surplus change onto the street.

Released, we breathe monoxide air where
sky is carbonised by dusk. The homeless
crouch in doorways, endure days designed
to strip the kernel from the husk.

HEIRLOOMS

A pearl, she said, *draws all things*
to itself. And she held them knotted
in her fingers the way mushrooms
glow in the roots of trees at dusk.

I thought of a pearl's intimacies:
a diver's blood hurtling in his lung,
the song, tidal in a singer's throat,
that faint pulse basking at her hands.

A pearl which is an oyster's tumour –
the plank in its blurred eye – globes with
breath's mist of adoration or envy.
I wanted to say: *Don't die. Not yet*.

Those evenings at the Steinway her voice
trembled up minor scales, brimming with
a song's old, burnished hurt then resting
in the black velvet of her sleep.

Once she saw these broken in the street,
scattered to the gutter, a surprising hail
I gathered up then re-strung on her
clavicle's fine harp; none lost, not one.

Watching the sea that last time, she said:
The waves are loose pearls, jostling.
And I paused, wanting to say how the sea
is the mind's irritant, how memory is a

pearl held then let go of, falling and
turning less brightly. But I said
nothing, watching her neck turn back
to the waves' quiet exclamations.

GEESE FROM A TIMBER HOUSE

That summer house. Its veranda and pitch-
pine frame, cracked windows, slant walls,
shot-up carpet straddling the stairs,
the smell of damp and pre-war family
holidays still seasoning each room.

Long days: reading, writing, watching the tide
trying to tear away the beach, rearing where
scores of geese steered south before the gales.
All over England rivers overflowed, the
railways had packed up and you were

travelling towards me, stranded on a train
with no real notion where I was. A borrowed
beach-house, that's all. The cuffs of my jumper
catching at a page, a coffee pot branding the table
like the thought of you, that we'd be together

and everything alright again, despite
those gales, the flypast of geese foretelling
worse to come. I wandered by each window,
hearing tiny shrieks of wind, watching
bushes tear their hair, and felt alive

with loneliness, wanting to mark a vee of
kisses in that favourite place behind your knee.
Then you rang and I was gunning the car
through floods to meet you at Saxmundham –
that fly-speck dotted on the map.

Night dropped. Tracks glittered into rain.
The train came late. Each mile of B road to
the coast was fraught with wind, high water,
fallen trees; then village lights shrank the dark
and I was opening our door into a stale

summer-scented past. We slept in its memory,
woke to calmer seas, to geese planing waves,
Landrovers braked in the road, serious men
gathered in Wellingtons and woollen hats,
their fingers stroking walnut stocks.

We sidled through them for our walk,
trudged two miles through spray and shingle,
deafened by the sea. It was later, hunched over
whisky macs, the gas-fire drying our shoes,
we heard the guns begin to talk.

PIANOFORTE

Big in the music business, our father
once kept thirteen pianos in the house.

People found this hard to believe, so we
pictured it for them: a house never short
of ivory or ebony, our fingers waltzing over
slave-trade arpeggios; a house where we
dined from the lid of a baby Broadwood,
skated to school on the Steinway's
borrowed castors, stood pianos on pianos –
the mini-piano inside the concert grand –
and at night whispered the scary German
consonants which captured sleep.

On winter evenings we lit candles in ornate
brass brackets, softening the rooms with
Edwardian light, with homesick songs of
patriotic loss, even employed a blind piano
tuner who only worked at night, each dawn
stepping over traps of snapped strings where
he'd tempered scales to pour cornflakes
or grill toast, the daylight he couldn't see
twisting down figured walnut legs.

My parents slept or argued or made love
on a Bechstein's broken sound-board, behind
a bedroom door of lacquered panels inlaid
with *fleur de lis*; how much of our childhood
was *pianissimo*, the timbre of felted hammers
falling, how much spent listening then, we never
say, hearkening for wrong chords to brood,
gather, darken the piano's terrible voice.

STREETLAMP LIZARD, DEIÀ

Each day, delirious with dusk,
I freeze into my deadly station,
crawl from the sun's split husk
to flex my tongue's dumb ululation.

My four feet sucker to the lamp
that lets aloof a faint green light;
my eyes, unblinking, press death's stamp
on moths that flicker from the night.

Unmoved by stars above the town
that's lit by traffic, human speech,
I prey until dawn draws me down
from where I cling, cold as a leech.

Then gods that spare me for this work
haunt azure skies as huge-eyed hawks.

REPORTAGE

The river running with its scut of foam,
that August of rain.

Nights in the car under cover of trees,
watching the road liquidise.

Taking down the weather's shorthand,
its stammering Derry brogue.

Gardens overgrown, cold-frames smashed,
a lace of cabbage leaf.

That neighbour chancing it, a newspaper
folded over his head.

Then one day of sun, drying out the evidence
of summer's ruin.

Drizzle hushing the ash of barbecues
left to cool at dusk.

A line of policemen swishing into grass,
re-run on the nightly news.

A bullet-hole in a blue temple *Wouldn't
think to harm a fly.*

Then more rain, weather's clichés falling,
its column inches being filed.

FROM THE PRESIDENTIAL SLEEP

Bell towers are tongueless, houses
crack and fall into the listless streets;
leaves whisper to themselves, windless
days store up abandoned heat.

Satellite dishes cup their ears, strain
towards the antic south; their wave-
lengths are scrambled consonants in
a lunatic's aphasic mouth.

A road runs over its own aftertaste:
creek-bottom salt, dried blood, bad luck.
Blizzards of crushed cement sift into
wind-screens on abandoned trucks.

Cats are wild for pigeons over sagging
roofs, dogs starve without a human hand;
dust-devils resurrect and whirl from
the suction of the land.

I'm guessing this, remembering my
dream of futures haunted by such fear,
the incubus of nothingness that cuckoos
out what's now and here.

I'm reaching towards unsplit rock,
clutching the crooked staff of speech;
quartz crystals shine, then dim, their
liquid moments trickling out of reach.

PROHIBITION

The day the booze ran out we tore
every copy of that banning order down,
that doomed decree flyposted across this
overheated, flyblown, stinking town.

At first an aspirin clarity, as if those
were the first unclouded thoughts
we'd ever had, then the slow scald of un-
quenched thirst blistering our throats.

Inventive, we drank thermometers,
distilled demijohns of pure methanol,
made solvent cocktails that left us
prophetically blind, but didn't kill.

Sightless, we sucked neon from
billboard lights, a Las Vegas Sling
that lifted us to pyrotechnic heights,
to miracles no alcohol could bring.

Then one visionary soul earthed himself
to the town's high-tension cables and we
got high on schooners of his piss, like
Berserkers in those fly agaric fables.

We got the taste for it alright, reclined
in bathtubs with curling toes, listening
to what the stars sobbed and sang to us
through submersed, mains-wired radios.

When the ban was lifted, every bar we
stumbled to seemed muzaked, placid.
Stuff vodka – we twirled zinc cocktail
stirrers in slammers of sulphuric acid.

Which, with votive insouciance
we tossed off neat, then clasping arms
flocked like inebriate, dusk-drawn bats to
the drunken celebration of the street.

Now cancered prostates have done for
almost all our dwindling club, Homeric piss-
artists who had the guts for sable brushes
to light the deathly static at life's hub.

New generations grow: when we're spark-out
on funeral biers, our black-gloved acolytes
will volley shots of liquid oxygen to cheer us
through eternal nights.

ACKNOWLEDGEMENTS

Poems selected here have appeared in the following collections:

A Country On Fire (Littlewood Press, 1986)

Sky Burial (Dangaroo Press, 1989)

Snow From the North (Dangaroo Press, 1992)

Circular Breathing (Dangaroo Press 1997)

A Night on the Lash (Seren 2004)

Poems selected here have been published in literary magazines, journals and anthologies and broadcast on radio programmes as follows:

Acumen, The Anglo-Welsh Review, Arts Yorkshire, Books & Poetry (BBC Radio 4), *BBC English* (BBC Radio 3), *Between the Ears,* (BBC Radio 3), *Pick of the Week* (BBC Radio 4), *Boomerang, Dhana, Dreamcatcher, The Edinburgh Review, Footnotes* (Schools Poetry Association), *The Forward Book of Poetry 2004, High, The Gregory Poems 1985-6* (Penguin), *The Independent on Sunday, Image, The Interpreter's House, Iron, Kunapipi, Radio Lancashire, Lancaster Literature Festival Anthology 1985, Lines Review, Moving Worlds, National Poetry Competition Anthology 1987, Neighbours* (Peterloo Poets), *The North, The Nottingham Collection* (5 Leaves Publications), *Not Just a Game* (5 Leaves Publications), *The Observer Review, Orbis, Orogenic Zones* (Bretton Hall Mountaineering Festival) *Outposts, Pennine Tracks* (Pennine Poets), *Pitch, Poetry Book Society Anthology, Poets' England 18* (Headland), *Poetry News, Poetry Review, Poetry Wales, Pretext, Raven, The Rialto, Scratch, Sheaf, Singing Brink, Smith's Knoll, Speaking English* (5 Leaves Publications), *Stand, Sunk Island Review, Tees Valley Writer, Times Literary Supplement, Westwords.*

A Country on Fire won a major Eric Gregory Award from the Society of Authors, **Circular Breathing** was a Poetry Book Society Recommendation.